Healing a nation: Leadership, Faith and Community in Haiti's Journey Forward

WADNER GEDEON

Copyright © 2024 Wadner Gedeon
All rights reserved.
ISBN: 9798343725797

NO PART OF THIS BOOK MAY BE REPRODUCED WITHOUT THE WRITTEN PERMISSION OF THE AUTHOR, WITH THE EXCEPTION OF BRIEF QUOTATIONS IN ARTICLES OR REVIEWS.

Sentinel Publishing
113 N. Union Ave
Lansdowne, PA 19050.

TABLE OF CONTENT

Autobiographie   3

History, Theology, Leadership,   7
and Community Leadership

Chapitre 1   21
What is Leadership?

Chapitre 2   50
The Leader in me

Chapitre 3
How to be an Effective Leader   78
     in Your Community?

Chapitre 4   118
10 Biblical models of community
     development

Chapitre 5   161
You Are Born to Lead!

Healing a nation: Leadership, Faith and Community in Haiti's Journey Forward

AUTOBIOGRAPHY

Greetings in the Name of Our Lord and Savior Jesus Christ!

I would like to take this opportunity to say "Thank you" to the Lord, Jesus Christ and to my friends and family for their support of the ministry. I have obeyed the voice of God and allowed the Holy Ghost to use me as a tool for His work. God has called me to minister to His people and has truly blessed me spiritually. Through this ministry, many souls have been added in the Kingdom of God. This time has been a learning process, full of trials and tribulations, but through the will of God it has been successful. I am one of many called to do the Lord's will, and I pray that I may find favor in His presence.

I was born in Haiti to Rev. Wilfrid Gedeon and Jumene Augustin on June 11. I have six brothers and six sisters, and the Lord has blessed me with my beautiful wife, Dr. Elizabeth Gedeon, whom I married September 15, 2007. At the time of my birth, my parents knew there was a God, but they had not yet offered themselves to Christ. However, as I was growing up, my parents devoted their lives to God and opened the doors for me. I attended church with some family members at the Free Methodist Church in Haiti, where I learned about Christ's love. Attend church was not all I did, though, because I was not saved. It wasn't until I came to the United States in the beginning of 1998 that I began to understand what Christ's love is about. I accepted Jesus as my savior when I was 16 years old at the Free Methodist Church of Bethlehem in Brooklyn, N.Y, founded by Rev. Joseph N. Pierre and Rev. Wilfrid Gedeon. Less than a year later, I was baptized and fully devoted my life to Christ. Jesus has anointed me with the power of the Holy Ghost and my life has been transformed forever. My preaching and evangelistic ministry had begun.

I attended Paul Robeson High School in Brooklyn, NY. I earned an Associate of Science in Telecommunication Technology Engineering from New York City College of Technology in 2004. I earned a B.A in Theology from Stanford Hill University School of Ministry in January 2004, and a Postgraduate Certificate in Mission organized by Together in Mission, from The Free Methodist Church School of Ministry in New Jersey; in association with Birmingham Christian College and Validated by the University of Wales in 2005.

I also completed a Bachelor of Arts in History & Education in 2005 from Touro College. I also hold a Master's Degree in Educational Technology at Touro College in 2007. Furthermore, I have a Master of Science Degree in School Administration & Supervision at Mercy College in May 2008. In addition, I also hold a postgraduate certificate in Teaching English to Speakers of Other Languages from Holy Family University in June 2009. In March 2022 I defended my dissertation and obtained my doctorate degree in leadership from American College of Education.

God has called me to His service since the day I accepted Him into my life. I have been serving the Lord faithfully for the past 27 years and nearly 22 years in pastoral ministries. He has given me the passion and the desire to reach out to those who do not know Him, and to those who are prisoners of Satan. God has used me to save lost souls and to give hope to those who are desperate. God has given me the vision to reach out to criminals, drug dealers, sex offenders, and atheists to come to Jesus Christ, and I will continue to work earnestly to accomplish this vision.

Additionally, I have been in education for the past 21 years, served as a teacher, data coordinator, 3 years as an assistant principal, and 9 years as a principal in the state of New Jersey.

My wife and I also have visions for this world. Together with Christ, we established our ministry, the New Generation Community Church in the Northeast section of Philadelphia, PA, and most recently this year we opened another campus in South Jersey to reach out to all people who wanted to be transformed and renewed with Christ. Satan is at work and is determined to destroy the people of this nation and around the world. It is time to help everyone understands his or her purpose in this world. We must safeguard the future of this country, Haiti, and people of all walks of life by using the spiritual weapons that God has given to us.

History, Theology, Leadership and Community Leadership

Introduction

Black Slavery and Haiti

The rich history of Haiti can be described as a journey of tragic and trying times, starting with the black slavery period and moving up to the present day, in which Haiti is labeled as the poorest country in the Western Hemisphere (Charles, 2020). Thus, the role of Haiti as the first black country that gained independence is interwoven with the legacy of slavery, and its impact is still felt to this day. Thus, Haiti was born as a black republic in 1804, the first independent state, through a successful slave revolt, yet this start was a mixed blessing (Alexander, 2021). The Haitian Revolution that made it free from the Europeans was a liberating event for black people in other Americas, but it was followed by more than two hundred years of isolationism, economic stagnation, and political turmoil.

Haiti, known as Saint-Domingue prior to the fight for independence, had one of the worst colonial ones in France, brutality included. In the sugar plantations, slaves were extensively used as labor and were killed through hard work, as most of the slaves died a few years after they reached America from Africa (Alexander, 2021).

These exploitations were systematic and formed the basis of many of the problems that are evident in Haiti's society today. The economy that was established based on slavery faced the challenge of transforming into a free labor economy, which was made worse by trade embargoes and the humiliating indemnity Haiti had to pay France for the liberation (Alexander, 2021). In the centuries since its revolution, Haiti has faced a seemingly endless series of crises: military takeovers, authoritarian rule, external force expeditions, and natural calamities, for that matter. The Haiti disaster in 2010, as a result of an earthquake that claimed more than a hundred thousand lives and rendered millions homeless and powerless, is an example of the country's susceptibility not only to natural disasters but also to societal structures that aggravate the effects of disasters (Johnson, 2021). Still, poverty, corruption, and instability remain critical issues in Haiti, as they do even today. The country faces enormous challenges in terms of its development and people's welfare.

The fact that the events in contemporary Haiti have a rich and complex background makes it rather important to prepare the new generation of leaders who would be able to consider the issue in the context of the globalizing world. Indeed, the global interdependence of today's world is such that Haiti's predicament cannot be addressed on its own. In this regard, leaders of countries should be sensitive to the rules governing the interaction of countries in the international community and be able to work within this framework on matters such as climate change and migration, among others (Johnson, 2021). Thus, people's unification for a common purpose in this context is rather complex. To begin with, there is a question of sensitization of Haitians and the rest of the world about the history of Haiti and, thus, present problems (Alexander, 2021). These findings could help promote understanding and support for Haiti's development interventions. Second, leaders have to establish confidence at the Haitian domestic level, both within different factions within the country who are often in opposition with each other. In this sense, leadership also means fostering Haiti's cultural endowment and the nation's people's tenacity as resources for growth. Thus, positive images introduce Haitian culture and accomplishments, which foster pride and unity that drive people to action. Additionally, mobilizing the global Haitian diaspora can help to introduce money, knowledge, and contacts, which are critical in development. In addition, it is crucial to involve the international community, NGOs, and the private sector in addressing Haiti's difficulties (Alexander, 2021). The leaders need to be diplomatic and have negotiation skills to be able to promote Haiti's agenda and interests on the international level while at the same time promoting cooperation and partnership. This includes questioning the conventional top-down aid paradigm and seeking to work for the sustainable capacity development of the target communities. In the Haitian context, uniting people for a noble cause means presenting a concept of development that would respond to the Haitian population's expectations and meet the country's ambitions in the distant future (Charles, 2020). It needs vision to envision hope and strategy in putting that hope into perspective with plans of change. Through the prevention and eradication of poverty and instability, building a sense of togetherness and pride, and participation in global society, a new generation of Haitian leaders can start to bring a new version to Haiti's historical narrative.

The Legacy of the Old Guard: Building Foundations and Holding Fast

The older generations, through their efforts, determination, and numerous triumphs, cannot be argued that they built the very foundation that the current world is built on. These individuals have gone through political crises, economic changes, and even social transformations, and so they hold a wealth of experience in their respective fields. They have set up key organizations, influenced people's perceptions, and created most of the liberties and chances found in today's youthful persons (Ciorciari, 2022). It has moved from civil rights movements to technological advancements, and the efforts of these old guards have defined the world people live in today. However, the same generation that has spent a lot of money to build these foundations seems to be very reluctant to hand over the baton to the next generation (Beckett, 2020). These include the belief that their experience is still valid and applicable to current events, as well as the loss of progress they have worked so hard to achieve.

The reluctance is evident in the various ways in which society is organized by different sections. In politics, one comes across politicians who have been in power for many years and do not want to let go, even if they are way past their prime. In business experienced managers may reject creative concepts developed by junior colleagues, relying on familiar procedures (Ciorciari, 2022). In community organizations and social movements, old guards may not easily relinquish power and give way for new brains to steer the course. The failure to let go of the reigns, as noble as this may be, can be disastrous for the community in attaining higher levels (Salam & Khan, 2020). It hinders creativity as anyone proposing a new way of doing things is discouraged, and instead, the organization continues to do things a certain way. This resistance can also result in leadership failing to capture new and growing trends in society, especially among the youthful population.

Additionally, by continuing to control power and positions, the older generation may contribute to non-appearing leadership positions for the younger people who actually can try to tackle them. This can result in a lack of succession in the skills pool to be able to fill leadership positions when the time arises. The dilemma, therefore, is how to pay deserving respect to the people whose advice and wisdom are so valuable to the society of the present and future generations while at the same time allowing them to chart their own course of destiny (Ciorciari, 2022). This change entails a change of attitude in both of these generational groups. The older generation has to understand that passing the torch is not like relinquishing their power or their throne; instead, they get to witness their ideas and their vision living on. In the meantime, younger generations have to be ready to hear what their forerunners have to say, respecting their own vision and view of reality (Beckett, 2020). In conclusion, elevating a community to a new level is an arduous task that has to bring together members of different ages. It proposes initiating solutions such as the establishment of successful mentorship and the presence of dialogue between generations, the acceptance of change, and the acknowledgment of the work done by those in the previous generations. For such goals, cooperation among the communities is the only way to maximize the usefulness of embodied expertise and innovativeness at the same time.

Generational Resistance: Obstacles to Passing the Baton

The transfer of power and authority from one generation to another is a common and inevitable feature inherent in any society's development. Exercising transition successfully despite its challenges tends to be difficult, especially regarding the shift of power from the older generations to the underbred (Naidu et al., 2021).

This feeling of gradual oblivion pushes them into asserting their control to hold on to what is still left of their importance. Thus, the idea of giving up the position is quite unappealing, as it means acknowledging that one's expertise is no longer required, which is a bitter pill for many individuals to swallow when their roles are tied to their identities. Closely related to this fear is the feeling that progress can be reverted or institutional knowledge may be transferred to the wrong hands if leadership is a tendency of frequent changes. Members of the older generation are likely to worry that young people are likely to make one mistake for another, seeing they have not undergone the same challenges that the current generation has undergone. It may result in the establishment of a mentality that the elders have to keep managing things out of benevolence, although they are going out of date (Naidu et al., 2021). Additionally, it is equally clear that pride and ego are some of the main factors that one has to deal with when it comes to generational succession. The leaders involved in the study spend several years and, in some cases, decades in charge of their respective domains, hence developing a feeling of ownership (Salam & Khan, 2020). Voluntary resignation is something that cannot be palatable, as it is equivalent to failure or even erasing one's identity. This is specifically so when one has attained significant accomplishments or fame in that occupation or specialty. Just the thought of becoming a figurehead or, even worse, irrelevant is psychologically unpalatable.

The next challenge is a clash of values and perspectives between different generations. Management of the older generation might not be able to embrace or endorse the techniques and goals of the younger generation. What looks like innovation to the young may look like foolishness or carelessness to the old (Salam & Khan, 2020). The generational difference in perception can foster mistrust; hence, the elders do not transfer powers to the young, who are seen as unfit or reckless (Naidu et al., 2021). Another factor pertains to financial issues, especially in companies and other business organizations. In a world in which people are working at the age of 65 and above, older persons may feel economic pressure to hold on to power because retirement or being out of power means no resources to depend on.

Finally, most organizations and institutions do not have a well-defined succession management model. If there is no proper channel for succession planning followed by training and development for the next generation, the old guards get disillusioned that there is no one qualified enough to replace them. The perceived lack of preparedness is a vicious cycle because the youth is locked out of positions that would afford them the experience and skills required to lead (Naidu et al., 2021) effectively. These challenges call for the deliberate effort of both generations to overcome them. It is one that encourages candid communication, respect for each other, flexibility, and the recognition of seniority (Salam & Khan, 2020). It is only when such barriers are effectively tackled that societies can provide for a seamless transition of power that is in the best interest of all citizens, young and old.

The Grip of Power: Elite Resistance to Generational Change

The lack of desire of elites, monarchs, and veteran leaders to pave the way for the new generation is a multifaceted process that manifests different psychological, social, and practical characteristics (Naidu et al., 2021). The form of resistance to change at the highest level in an organization or society has an elaborate effect of slowing down or even halting growth and development. At the center of this is the lure of power, plain and simple. These people have been in authority for a long time; they have become or are very possessive of the powers that they hold. This attachment can easily translate to a feeling that their rule is crucial, which leads to a feeling of entitlement to more time on the throne (Salam & Khan, 2020). At the center of this is the lure of power, plain and simple. These people have been in authority for a long time; they have become or are very possessive of the powers that they hold. This attachment can easily translate to a feeling that their rule is crucial, which leads to a feeling of entitlement to more time on the throne (Salam & Khan, 2020). The idea of handing over the reins becomes not just professionally daunting but threatening to one's being as a person and employee. This is due to fear being a major factor in this resistance. Leaders may have fears and doubts about how power will be utilized once they are out of power or how their status will change (Naidu et al., 2021). The fear attributable to their production is that one day, all their hard work and achievements shall be disassembled or even ignored by a new and younger generation with different needs and solutions. This fear can take the form of the so-called 'protection' where highly experienced executives convince themselves that they need to remain in charge to avoid any mistakes.

In many sectors, Haitians have positively impacted the United States and have enriched American culture. In government, Haitian Americans love Mia, who was the first black Republican woman to win a seat in the U.S. House of Representatives as the Representative of Utah from 2015 to 2019. Literature-wise, Haitian-American author Edwidge Danticat has written targeted novels and short stories that exaggerate the Haitian-American experience.

In many sectors, Haitians have positively impacted the United States and have enriched American culture. In government, Haitian Americans love Mia, who was the first black Republican woman to win a seat in the U.S. House of Representatives as the Representative of Utah from 2015 to 2019. Literature-wise, Haitian-American author Edwidge Danticat has written targeted novels and short stories that exaggerate the Haitian-American experience. In politics, Haitian Americans have been active, for instance, from Patrick Gaspard, the political director in the White House, to the Obama presidency (Naidu et al., 2021). In literature, Haitian-Americans like Edwidge Danticat and Roxane Gay have become prominent writers who write beautiful and touching literature that captures the Haitian-Americans' struggle for identity in their new country and the absence of their native country (Yi, 2021). Currently, Wyclef Jean and Rasin Banda have incorporated Haitian beats along with modern urban genres, making Haitian music more recognized throughout the world (Boutros, 2020). In the field of science and technology, Haitian Americans have significantly contributed to society. Yvonne Cagle, who is a NASA astronaut who advocates for diversity, has played a key role in the study of astronaut health and continues to work and assist as a space telemedicine consultant in the United States. Apart from the sentiments expounded herein, Haitian Americans are proving to be great assets across the fields as leaders in business, politics, and the arts, among others (Bhardwaj, 2022). They have fought hard and indeed brought diverse innovations into communities within the United States of America. The employment of Haitians proves that Haitians can be productive citizens of the United States and have the potential to bring positive change to society. There is the question of organizational culture as well. Called institutional theory, this theory posits that organizations tend to remain rigid as the status quo is usually hard to break. Most organizational power relationships in government, business, or other relevant systems are programmed to maintain the status quo. As the systems are well-developed organizations, the established leaders have a strong connection and association with them; hence, newcomers may find it hard to penetrate (Naidu et al., 2021). Culturally, such conflict can become pathological, as written above, where the absence of capacity of the young people to step up and be given more responsibilities becomes in itself an argument against the young people being given more responsibility (Beckett, 2020). Additionally, there is usually a sense of entitlement, which is best illustrated by the fact that most senior leaders truly believe that nobody else can do the job as they do. Many years in politics, society, or economy are capable of creating an attitude that only they can handle the challenge of leading the nation (Naidu et al., 2021). This is because this belief makes them close their eyes to the new and invigorating ideas that young leadership brings to any operation.

CHAPTER 1

What is Leadership?

According to Banks et al. (2022), the process of leading people to fulfill their common goal is known as leadership. Todnem (2021) views leadership as the ability to make choices and to be held accountable for all the decisions made. Banks et al. (2022) definition is oriented toward influence, whereas Todnem's (2021) view is primarily based on accountability. Leadership is not a position but a function of the influence one has over others and results in the generation of changes through the use of influence. Leadership is not limited to the rank structure that most of the time defines it and gives it a specific meaning. Thus, leadership can be discussed as a peculiar phenomenon that takes different forms and occurs in various contexts in today's fast-changing environment (Banks et al., 2022).

    The biblical model of leadership, as demonstrated by Jesus Christ, is a servant-leadership that involves serving others and laying down one's life for others. True leadership, as portrayed by Jesus Christ washing his disciples' feet in John 13:1–17, entails putting others first (King James Version, 2019). He encourages people, especially leaders, to care for others, listen to them kindly, and set a good example, shown through humility and commitment to ethics.

One of the most crucial factors of leadership is the vision. Leaders have dispositions that enable them to look at the present situation not only as it is but as it could be improved. They can communicate it and be willing to let the passion and desire for the vision build among the people (Ospina et al., 2020). This visionary quality equips the leaders with the ability to chart a course and create meaning for the people who are being led. Through a vision leaders provide a vision of what can be achieved, hence encouraging people to work hard and fight through harsh times. Decision-making is another of the basic leadership competencies. Specialists also note that leaders always find themselves in a kind of dilemma that needs a great deal of consideration and planning (Gardner et al., 2020). They have to analyze a situation or an event, think of implications, and decide on a course of action based on the vision and values system. Every manager knows that the role of decision-making is not in searching for the perfect solution to a problem but in readiness to take certain risks and apply lessons learned in resolving the problem.

Leadership is incomplete without communication. Communication also presents itself as another indispensable requisite for leaders, where the latter must be in a position to influence the way their subordinates perceive them, the tasks assigned, or the feedback that has been given (Gardner et al., 2020). They have to learn how to lose their dominant gender communication ways in order to win over the target population and have them comprehend it and act on it if need be (Banks et al., 2022). Apart from being articulate, good leaders should also be good listeners. They establish conditions that allow people to discuss issues and listen to one another to establish what is primarily important. Leadership entails the concept of interaction (Ospina et al., 2020). Managers also know that developing good relations with subordinates, organizational stakeholders, and other members of the public is essential. This is because they spend time and effort studying the followers' requirements, desires, and goals.

The concept of leadership has changed over time due to changes in leadership definitions and theories. Thinking about leadership in the past was mainly associated with the ability to command, control, and make decisions on behalf of others. However, from the perspective of the new forms of leadership, collaboration, sharing, and empowerment are regarded as priorities. Contemporary leaders are those who are able to develop the personal responsibility and coordination abilities of the employees introduced to the situation (Pellegrini et al., 2020). Ethics and integrity are also strongly related to leadership. One might agree with the assertion that leaders are expected to be an example for the people in the organization or the society at large. Ethical leadership can be defined as the responsibility of making the right moral choices, being open and timely in one's actions, and bearing the consequences (Ospina et al., 2020). When leaders are role models of integrity, employees will emulate this, and this will help encourage honesty and stop the buck stops.

      To be more precise, leadership can be regarded as one of the key factors that influence culture and performance within organizations. Formerly, very often, they define what is appropriate or suitable conduct in a particular situation and determine the rules of the organization's functioning. They generate conditions that either promote change and development or that stifle change and development. It is quite crucial to have an organizational culture in any organization, and competent leaders embrace this by influencing it to suit their strategic plans. The very nature of leadership, as a subject, does not remain confined to a particular paradigm and set of principles; it is a dynamic process that demands constant learning in order to be effectively applied at all levels of organizational hierarchy (Pellegrini et al., 2020). Leadership issues are dynamic in nature, meaning that issues facing leaders are bound to change due to technological developments, the global economy, and social factors. Effective managers only need to adopt the growth approach, which involves looking for ways to gain new skills or new experiences that would be beneficial to leadership (Ospina et al., 2020). They retain an opportunity to listen and are willing and able to change their strategy based on information and occurrences. While leadership is local in a way, meaning that it has tentacles in the specific areas of operation, the effects of leadership percolate throughout the organization and even beyond (Todnem, 2021). Leaders are able to influence societies, promote social development, and transform stakeholders's lives. One must not forget that leaders are present in history, and they have shifted the course of nations, reinvented industries, and motivated people. On the other hand, there are real-life horrific examples of the things that leaders do that bring calamities, which points to the fact that leadership positions come with great accountability.

Leadership, on the other hand, entails the facilitation of people's performance and the encouragement of people to transform the existing systems for the better. It involves the skills of constructive self-assertion and self-effacement, idealism and realism, stubbornness, and versatility (Banks et al., 2022). Managers must be in a position to understand different difficulties while continuing to expand on the organizational vision and mission. Leaders must build confidence, encourage people to work together and establish conditions in which each person and organization can unleash their potential. Finally, leadership is the process of leading others for the benefit of all without focusing on achieving personal benefits like authoritarianism, material gains, and political consolidation (Ospina et al., 2020). It concerns the full abilities of people and teams, providing them with the direction to achieve organizational or corporate goals. In business, politics, education, and many more fields, leadership has the potential to change the quality of lives, institutions, and entire societies (Pellegrini et al., 2020). Thus, in the constant increase in the importance of the global challenges that mankind has to solve, it is crucial to have strong ethical and visionary leaders. Although leadership can be described as complex, it is very important for each person to know what leadership entails so as to be able to cultivate the appropriate character and personality that is required in leadership in the modern world today.

The Characteristics of Effective Leadership

Effective leadership can be described as the ability to influence people's actions toward developing and completing key tasks. However, it is important to distinguish that there are a number of general traits that are correlated with effective leaders, no matter the type of organization and the sphere of business (Bhardwaj, 2022). These are the characteristics that shape successful leadership and, in turn, influence the outcomes of organizations and groups. Leadership is one of the organizational management systems that involve various qualities, one of which is vision (Benmira& Agboola, 2021). Leaders have to acknowledge what is beyond vision and can picture how things will be in the future. Others are able to express this vision in a manner that would motivate people and thus provide a focus and direction. Great managers set up goals and expectations that go beyond a specific individual, group, or organization to motivate people to work for the attainment of long-range goals. The type of thinking and describing of the desired end-state is very central in charting the course of an organization and inspiring people to actualize it.

Teachers and principals should have the qualities of instructional leadership. They act to effectively define achievement standards for curriculum and student performance and conduct research. Effective principals coordinate with the teachers to ensure that there is a well-developed curriculum and assessment maps complementary to high standards. They support specific training and development for educators in order to facilitate their professional growth with regard to classroom practices. School principals also observe lessons with keen interest while observing the mandate to advise teachers on how they can improve their lessons (Porfírio et al., 2020). High-performing teachers, on the other hand, use assessment results to review their approach to the topic to be taught and adjust their classroom methods to accommodate as many students as possible (Fries et al., 2020). Due to this shared professional practice and utilization of data, exceptional instructional leaders foster the improvement of students' performance.

Instructional principals are also important fixtures in the learning process since they influence the student's performance. Instructional leadership entails a wide range of initiatives and the use of effective micro-communication skills, focused instructional leadership vision, and practices that embrace academic standards and high expectations for teachers and students. Observance of classroom instructions is done frequently, which results in detailed feedback given to the teachers with regard to the reinforcement of the teaching. As for the curricular and evaluative aspects, instructional principals also make adequate curriculum and assessment charts available and support the provision of constructivist professional development programs to enhance the teachers' instructional practices regularly (Porfírio et al., 2020). Some possible vectors in this relation include elements such as communication skills, the focus of the instructional leader on data and evidence, as well as the capacity to foster trust and cooperation among the staff. While managerial leaders dedicate their attention to activities such as budgeting and conformance, instructional leaders' concentration lies in teaching and learning (Fries et al., 2020). The similarities are found in the requirement of both managerial and leadership qualities. These are essential competencies that effective principals use in an appropriate manner to promote the right culture in the school to support students' achievement. In this case, principals can ensure that the management and leadership in their communities produce the best results for all learners if only some approaches are implemented strategically.

The concept of emotional intelligence has emerged as a critical component of leadership skills in organizations. Emotional intelligence involves the ability to control one's own emotions as well as the ability to understand the emotions of others (Porfírio et al., 2020). They are proficient in interpersonal communications, conflict resolution, and maintaining good employee relations. Leaders possessing interpersonal emotional intelligence are capable of handling relationships' complexity and building organizational trust. It promotes understanding the feelings of other people in the organization and increases team members' cooperation, thus improving organizational performance. It is, therefore, evident that integrity is a core component of leadership that gives it its standard foundation.

Adaptability is yet another competency that is essential in leadership roles. Thus, today's leaders need to understand that the world is full of uncertainties, and one needs to embrace change. Thus, they are adaptive and ready to synchronize their strategies and actions to achieve maximum impact. Flexible executives are open to change, bring new ideas to an organization, and promote experimenting with different solutions. More important still is the ability to change and adapt in light of some circumstances that might pose a threat to the existence of the organization or the continued success of the business ventures undertaken (Fries et al., 2020). Fearlessness is the core competency of top managers; they need to make the right choices and sometimes take risks. A good leader can easily make decisions that make them unpopular or contradict past decisions, and they have the ambition to drive big changes and the tenacity to power through the challenges (Gardner et al., 2020). Fearless people make the impossible possible by motivating those around them to go the extra mile. This ability to embrace risk and to boldly engage in these challenges is often the hallmark of leaders from the rest.

One can argue that the ability to empower others is one of the core leadership traits. In this case, leaders are fully aware of the potential of subordinates as well as try to foster their development (Gardner et al., 2020). They assign tasks, offer promotions, and give people what they need to feel that they are wanted in the organization. Thus, leaders encourage the delegation of certain tasks, as this entails people's ability and willingness to commit themselves to the achievement of goals (Gardner et al., 2020). It also helps in the overall capacity building of the organization and increases the competency of the individual at the workplace. Clearly, another of the significant components of leadership is decisiveness. Managers and leaders are always placed in quandaries that call for timely and competent decisions. They are able to obtain and process necessary data and look at the problem from different angles to decide on actions that are in conformity with personal values and visions (Fries et al., 2020). Leaders are to be decisive when managing their subordinates or coming up with solutions, especially when the situation is foggy or complicated. Another critical attribute is the ability to make decisive and sometimes nuclear choices and then proceed confidently to execute the decisions made.

Ideally, passion and enthusiasm are some of the defining

characteristics that compel others to take collective action. Leaders are, therefore, very passionate about the vision they have for the organization, and they also have to be passionate about their role (Fries et al., 2020). They are energetic and committed to what they do, as this generates a good attitude towards work, which others are compelled to emulate. This can be something great to have because it can be used, for example, in countering adversities or in keeping the team's spirits up during problem-solving. Continuing learning is a disposition that enhances one's ability to remain relevant despite rising changes in the social context. In general, effective managers and other organizational-level employees possess the ability to learn and seek development purposes. They seek feedback, analyze situations that took place, and do their best in order to develop themselves. This focus on training and development does not only benefit themselves but is also highly motivational for other employees as it encourages the everlasting improvement of one's own performance within the company. The concept of resilience can be viewed as a valuable leadership attribute that enables managers to cope with adversities. Leadership effectiveness is characterized by mental resilience and resilience after failure (Bhardwaj, 2022). They have positive attitudes and focus on how they can make use of the difficulties in life as good learning experiences. 'Strong' leaders encourage their followers and do not leave their subordinates abandoned during hard times. This feature implies a sustainable and steady further strive in the course of exercises set to persistently achieve high results and act in hard conditions.

In summary, leadership is one of the most important factors in any organization, as it includes all the personal attributes, skills, and behaviors that allow people to facilitate the achievement of objectives. Although none of these characteristics can be naturally found in a leader to the fullest extent, the leader must be constantly striving to enhance the mentioned qualities (Gardner et al., 2020). Thus, making commitments, establishing specific goals, understanding mistakes, and seeking solutions can help a leader establish structures that change for the better and bring success to the organizational environment (Benmira& Agboola, 2021). Thus, the outlined characteristics stand as the essential prerequisites for success in leadership, as the challenges of leadership remain constant, but their manifestation may be significantly different.

Leadership Styles

Leadership styles pertain to the specific patterns of behaviors that leaders employ in leading their subordinates. It is important to understand that these styles largely depend on the personality of the leader, the type of organization, the context, and the members of the team who are being led. It is essential to comprehend various leadership styles since it will help leaders adjust to the situation and be more effective in their work. Arguably, the most famous typology of leadership behaviors was introduced by psychologist Kurt Lewin in the 1930s (Endrejat& Burnes, 2022). Lewin identified three primary leadership styles: Autocratic, democratic, and laissez-faire leadership styles (Endrejat& Burnes, 2022). The autocratic leadership style, also referred to as the authoritarian leadership style, involves the leader giving clear direction and authority. Autocratic leaders are the ones who make all the decisions without consulting their employees, colleagues, or subordinates. Supervisors establish achievable goals and are vigilant in measuring results (Kump, 2023). The style proves useful in scenarios where prompt decisions are expected or when working with new employees who require a great deal of supervision. Nevertheless, it can cause low morale, low creativity, and high turnover if used frequently.

      Participative or democratic leadership entails encouraging team members to participate in decision-making processes. Democratic leaders seek cooperation from their team and allow ideas to be proposed and discussed (Kump, 2023). The leader is the final authority in the team, but before making any decision, they consult their subordinates. Haitian people are very warm and friendly; the family unit is extremely valued, as are the community-oriented aspects of the island citizens. Haitians are proud of their African, French, and Caribbean heritage. Several attributes have been distilled from the political instability as well as economic woes of Haiti, and they have contributed to higher levels of distrust that subordinates hold for authority figures. However, when applying the participative and democratic leadership styles, one should bear these cultural variations in mind. Leaders may find themselves in a position where they will have to consider the importance of power distance when it comes to implementing more vivid communication and equal opportunities for speaking (Endrejat& Burnes, 2022). This way, the Haitian communities can develop participative leadership since it is informed by trust, consistency, and constructive interdependence.

Following Lewin's work, other researchers and theorists have noted other leadership types that correspond to the realities of today's organizations and management. One such model is the full-range leadership theory, which was developed by Bernard Bass and Bruce Avolio, and it consists of transformational leadership, transactional leadership, and passive-avoidant leadership (Kanat-Maymon et al., 2020). Some of its features include leaders that mobilize others to go beyond their own self-interest in the interest of the organization. These leaders present a clear and inspiring vision and act as a reference point and mentor for their direct reports whilst engaging with them at the individual level and encouraging their employees' higher-order thinking processes. A key trait that distinguishes transformational leaders from other types of leaders is the emphasis on the promotion of followers' growth and improvement, as well as on the congruence of individual and organizational objectives (Siangchokyoo et al., 2020). The style is most suitable in processes that require change within an organization and for the creation of new ideas. Transactional leadership, on the other hand, deals with the exchange that is going to happen between the leaders and the followers. Transactional leaders define the expectations for subordinates and the consequences of meeting or failing to meet these expectations when they prescribe certain rewards to be given once goals are achieved or punishments to be inflicted once goals are not achieved (Viana Feranita et al., 2020). Such structures use order as their main principle, communication, and performance control. Although it may help retain the status quo and bring order to keep subordinates on track in accomplishing tangible objectives, it can be less motivated and less innovative as compared to transformational leadership.

Passive-avoidant leaders do not provide leadership at all; all their attributes are negative, and they are also known as 'hands-off' leaders. It is somewhat similar to laissez-faire leadership; however, it generally arises from delegation by neglect or abstention (Tayfur Ekmekci et al., 2021). For example, passive avoidant leaders may ignore the need to offer direction, appraisal, or encouragement to subordinates, and this results in low productivity and morale among the workforce. Another widely-known model of leadership behavior is the Six Emotional Leadership Styles, defined by Daniel Goleman (Afrifa Jnr &Dzogbewu, 2020). These are visionary leadership, coaching leadership, affiliative leadership, democratic leadership, pacesetting leadership, and commanding leadership, as provided by Goleman (Afrifa Jnr &Dzogbewu, 2020). Strategic leaders motivate a number of other people and possess a clearly expressed vision and a set of directions. Coaching managers work to enhance the team member's competencies and optimize the achievement of organizational goals through individual support. Affiliative leaders devote a lot of effort to ensuring that there is no conflict while at the same time ensuring that the members of the team have developed close relationships. Democratic leaders, like Lewin's approach to democratic behavior, promote the participation of subordinates in the decision-making process (Banks et al., 2022). Pacesetting leaders demand and model the correct execution of an activity, thereby provoking performance and initiative from followers. Authoritative leaders, like autocratic leadership styles, make decisions, and these are communicated to the subordinates to be followed as planned. According to Goleman, the greatest leaders are equally competent in applying varying behavioral patterns, hence the suitability of the title as situational leaders.

There are a number of leadership styles that have evolved in light of the current organizational structures and society. Servant leadership focuses on a leader's manner of providing help and support to the subordinates and taking an interest in their development and well-being while translating the trust from followers (Pawar et al., 2020). Authentic leadership is centered on the leader's pursuit of genuine and genuine relationships with others where the leader is real and genuine, in addition to being aware of himself or herself and showcasing ethical character to the followers (Chen &Sriphon, 2022). Adaptive leadership is focused on the leader's capacity to assist organizations in coping with complicated problems and flux within environments and fosters exploration, growth, and shared inquiry. Distributed leadership suggests that leadership is not the domain of a single person; instead, the responsibility is distributed throughout the team members and gives impact value to each team member's input (Todnem, 2021). Situational leadership is a theory that was introduced by Paul Hersey and Ken Blanchard. It asserts that a manager should adjust the leadership style according to the experience or the level of development of the followers, and this theory offers four types of leadership, including directing, coaching, supportive, and delegating, and the kind of leadership depends on the organization and the employee (Wuryani et al., 2021). All these leadership styles have benefits and may include the following drawbacks and advantages, depending on the situation. There are elements of the organization, including the organizational culture and the existing team, the type of activity that is to be performed, and the existing top, that influence the most appropriate leadership style. Some of the successful leadership styles involve the ability of a leader to be completely versatile in their approach to leadership in the setting and among people. They understand that no one can employ a particular type of behavior and get the best results at all times and that the best managers are those who are able to switch between the two, depending on the circumstances.

The knowledge of all these leadership styles and their uses is very important in the molding of leaders. From the analysis of the strategies, leaders can reach a conclusion on which approach is more constructive for a specific situation by appreciating the merits and demerits of both options (Wuryani et al., 2021). Finally, without a doubt, the best leaders are situational, or worse, transformational-transactional, meaning that they can select from the largest number of styles to use in a given situation with the maximum efficiency of staff and organizational performance (Todnem, 2021). Given that organizations and societies in today's world are progressively changing, flexibility to work in different contexts of leadership will always create room for leaders in different fields of work.

Are Leaders Born or Made?

Leadership has been a topic of great interest for decades, and one of the most intriguing topics has always been whether leaders are born or made. This nature versus nurture debate that exists in leadership offers very important consequences in terms of leadership management and development. Experiencing the issue, most people attempt to find the dispassionate answer: while there are many arguments in the debate, it is probable that for everybody, leadership skills are probably both inherent and acquired (Siangchokyoo et al., 2020). The 'leaders are born' theory suggests that people are predestined to lead by virtue of instilled attributes or qualities. Those who support this view try to give examples of great leaders who were born with the gift of mobilizing people throughout their lifetime (Todnem, 2021). They contend that certain characteristics like charisma, confidence, and decision-making capacity are part of a person's DNA and, therefore, untrainable once one lacks such traits

(Song et al., 2022). The idea is backed up by some research carried out in behavioral genetics, which hints that some aspects of personality related to leadership, for example, extraversion and openness have a genetic basis.

In addition, Song et al. (2022) have established that leadership role occupancy—the degree to which persons fill leadership positions—is heritable for twins as well as adopted children. These findings give some degree of plausibility to the belief that there could be a 'leadership gene' or a series of genetics that make some people more suited to leadership roles. The reasoning behind this is the belief that such people are gifted with the natural ability to influence, encourage, and direct others, which makes them preferable in leadership positions (Todnem, 2021). However, the 'leaders are made' point of view assumes that leadership is a process that consists of a definite number of skills and desirable behaviors that can be taught and acquired to various extents (Siangchokyoo et al., 2020). This can be judged by the huge number of leadership development programs, training courses, and curricula for improving leadership skills. Based on this view, it is asserted that there are genetic predispositions to leadership, but other important leadership assets and skills may be learned in a given field, a specific course, and practice (Wuryani et al., 2021). In this view, leadership can be born or made, as can be observed from the biblical teachings. Although Moses complained to God and doubted He could use him for such a purpose (Exodus 4:10–13), God made him a powerful leader (King James Version, 2019). Likewise, David was anointed as a young shepherd and grew to be a mighty king of Israel. Such examples indicate that some leaders may have innate qualities, though they can be developed through divine guidance and experience.

Additionally, it indicates that the pace at which the world is transforming means that leaders cannot afford to stop learning and growing. The leadership competencies that are necessary today do not tally with those needed in today's leadership due to the dynamic nature associated with globalization and technological advancement. It is good evidence to stress that leadership is a process that requires a constant acquisition of learnings and improvement of competence rather than in-born talents (Wuryani et al., 2021). In today's leadership literature, there is a more balanced and widespread understanding of the fact that genetics, as well as the environment, interactively influence leadership qualities (Siangchokyoo et al., 2020). The view says that there are certain abilities in some people that help in leadership but that the abilities alone cannot make people great leaders. They offer a starting point on which the leadership competencies may be developed over time in the context of practice, learning, and training.

The balanced view does not deny that there may be hereditary components to some of the personality traits and cognitive abilities that make people good leaders. For instance, society has admitted that aspects such as affective stability, perceived openness, and general intelligence have both hereditary and leadership correlations and performance implications. However, the manifestation of these traits and the ways in which people bring them to work and showcase them in leadership positions are affected by environmental variables such as nurture, schooling, culture, and past experiences (Todnem, 2021). Additionally, this view asserts that, while people may be born leaders, such potentials need to be nurtured to really count. Inexperienced or born talent alone does not guarantee successful leadership; therefore, they ought to apply knowledge, skill, and experience to produce a good outcome (Wuryani et al., 2021). The view is similar to the perspective of leadership as a continuous learning process, where one increases one's leadership ability throughout one's life.

The concept that 'leaders are made' in addition to 'born' also reflects the influence of situational processes in leadership selection and success (Wuryani et al., 2021). It is possible that in different situations and in relation to different problems, other leadership competencies are needed. This paper, therefore, clearly shows, for example, that while a certain individual may be only good at leading in one particular situation or setting, he or she may be completely poor at leading in another setting, something that underscores the need for leadership development to be a lifelong process, hence the need for leadership training (Song et al., 2022). Such a conclusion poses certain consequences for leadership development practices, as such a paradigm represents a balanced approach. From it, one can deduce that although one should appreciate and promote natural-born leaders, the world should spend a lot of money on training and developing leaders in individuals (Fries et al., 2020). It promotes the leadership effectiveness of a wider population, not just of the individuals who have the 'prototypical' quality of a leader from childhood (Bhardwaj, 2022). Additionally, this perspective raises awareness of cultivating contexts for leadership to happen. Supervisory groups can also be effectively utilized by organizations and societies to help people develop leadership skills by giving them a chance to lead and gain experience; possible failures may be corrected through discussions or consultations with mentors (Chen &Sriphon, 2022). The approach can also contribute to the creation of a broad field of leadership, the representatives of which possess distinct skills and different visions of the world, which is especially valuable in today's world.

Understanding that leadership is hereditary and acquired dramatically affects the educational systems, practices of organizations, and the entire society in building leadership. This understanding implies that leadership should be included right from the learning curriculum, especially in educational institutions (Siangchokyoo et al., 2020). There is no reason for schools and universities to rely on ability tests alone to find natural-born leaders; everybody should be encouraged to take on leadership roles in order to develop their leadership potential in such projects as group assignments and projects that are targeted at benefiting society (Song et al., 2022). Besides, this approach not only assists in the development of leadership qualities of those who could be potentially regarded as leaders but also helps all the participants of the process to become leaders, as far as deep inside each of them, there is a latent leader.

Finally, it remains to be remembered that the discussion of the origin of leaders still remains relevant, but currently, the concepts that form the basis of successful leadership can be called both innate and acquired talents. It is sometimes possible to note that certain people are born leaders, but even these people cannot become managers without proper training. Leadership skills can also be stated as the process of improving the skills, gaining experience, and allowing for adaptation to different contexts and scenarios (Benmira& Agboola, 2021). The described perspective for leadership has a significant impact on the expectations related to leadership development at personal and societal levels (Bhardwaj, 2022). It inspires people's attitude towards leadership, and everyone is welcome to change and become a leader someday. This also reaffirms the need to open leadership development opportunities to diverse people, as it emerges from the research that someone in a certain role may produce a leader when given a chance (Fries et al., 2020).

CHAPTER 2

The Leader in Me

'The Leader in Me' can be characterized as a revolutionary concept of self- and leadership development that started to become popular relatively recently. This philosophy, which entails the belief that everyone has the potential to be a leader since the aptitudes of a leader reside in each person, opposes the presumptions of leadership with the delegation of authority. However, it posits that leadership is a behavioral disposition that can be learned in a person at any given time, regardless of the individual's age, culture, or social class (Pellegrini et al., 2020). In essence, 'The Leader in Me' is focused on helping every learner to be in control of their destiny, make good decisions, and impact the community in a positive manner (Fries et al., 2020). It is useful since this approach changes the position from the external locus of control and stress to the internal locus of control and action-taking.

The roots of 'The Leader in Me' can largely be traced back to the work and ideas originally formulated by Stephen Covey, the author of the book 'The 7 Habits of the Highly Effective People'.

Covey's ideas were translated into an educational concept by educators and school leaders who saw a chance for these values to infiltrate the school, beginning with the children themselves (Covey, 2004). From there, the philosophy grew and enveloped various areas of human life, starting with business organization, community development, and self-improvement processes (Kanat-Maymon et al., 2020). Organizational culture is where the 'The Leader in Me' approach stands out as a great strength because it does not focus on just the children. In contrast with most other educational processes, it does not only teach choices for the acquisition of specific skills or the achievement of certain results; it seeks to mold the total personality. Thus, this approach covers numerous aspects of educational development, such as emotional intelligence, goal setting, time management, and interpersonal and ethical skills (Fries et al., 2020). Through developing such different aspects of the personality, 'The Leader in Me' contributes to children becoming successful members of society who are ready to face modern challenges.

Another key component of 'The Leader in Me' concept is individual responsibility. It promotes personal responsibility in that people are free to make decisions, and arising from it, they assume the risk of the foregoing decisions. The importance of accountability as a value that is being nurtured is enlightening because it serves as an indication to people of their capacity to assume control over their own lives rather than be victims of their environments (Tench et al., 2021). It engulfs a concept of a problem-solving perspective where people are always in search of opportunities to effect and initiate change and enhance the quality of their lives or their communities' quality of life. This is typically true because execution of 'The Leader in Me' practices sometimes starts with an assessment of the self. Personals should reflect on their own values, assets, liabilities, and long-term objectives (Villares et al., 2023). The introspective process creates the basis for learning and an alternative for leaders' development. Self-organization, in this context, implies acquiring knowledge about individuals so as to make more conscious decisions based on vital values and goals.

One of the most crucial facets of the 'The Leader in Me' model is self-leadership, which means that leadership begins with the self. This form of leadership includes hard work, learning how to control one's feelings, establishing and realizing individual objectives, as well as personal growth (Tench et al., 2021). The justification is that people cannot be managers to other individuals without proving that they can manage their lives. Not only does this focus on self-leadership equip a person with skills to function in a higher hierarchical rank, but it also provides them with tools to be a constructive influence in their daily interpersonal relationships. Nearly all of the approaches and principles outlined in 'The Leader in Me' also pay great attention to the growth mindset element (Villares et al., 2023). This requires making and promoting the attitude that people's capabilities are expandable through practice and training processes. A growth mindset leads people to welcome difficulties, keep on trying even when faced with failure, labor to increase their capabilities through practice, acknowledge and learn from constructive feedback, and draw strengths from other people's successes. This is a useful outlook to develop for a person, as it molds him for further self-improvement as well as for the general well-being that comes with positive thinking.

One more essential aspect of the 'The Leader in Me' concept is interpersonal skills. Leadership is not the process of focusing on one's own success alone but, instead, the ability to make a difference in other people and to coordinate them. To this end, the approach focuses on skills like listening, understanding the feelings of others, communication, conflict-solving, and collaboration (Jones, 2022). These are relationship skills that prepare people to make great interpersonal relations, teamwork skills that prepare one to work under different teams, and change skills that prepare one to change development in society positively (Tench et al., 2021). An implementation of some of the concepts taught in 'The Leader in Me' is mainly focused on goal setting to achieve fulfilling objectives. Thus, this functional approach contributes to the creation of purpose and direction in life. Thus, it can help in learning the processes of dividing the overall goals into steps, how to prioritize and keep up with the goals, and motivation even in the long run. In this way, people get specific experience and skills in planning, time management, and determination.

It is worth noting that one of the most constructive features of 'The Leader in Me' is that it creates a ripple effect. When people adopt these principles, positive change occurs, and those people turn into great leaders and impact the people around them. Hence, it can cause a transformation not only in the lives of people or within the lives of people but also within communities (Kanat-Maymon et al., 2020). Schools that administer 'The Leader in Me,' for example, tend to note enhanced performance, cultural shifts, behavior, and parental engagement (Jones, 2022). Hence, it is essential to underline that 'The Leader in Me' is not an application of easy solutions or non-profound work with children. It is a change in attitudinal direction as well as a change in behavior, as it can take a lot of time and practice to change a habit. The process of leadership development can be unending, but there is always time in a leader's life to learn new leadership skills and improve on the existing skills.

Therefore, it is important to conclude that 'The Leader in Me' provides a great and helpful program for working on success and leadership in individuals (Jones, 2022). It promotes self-awareness, responsibility at the personal level, the importance of a positive approach, and other competitive interpersonal skills that allow a person to be a positive agent of change at the individual level and in society at large (Tench et al., 2021). Hence, as this philosophy is instituted and developed further, there is hope for the molding of the next generation of leaders who will be adequately equipped to meet the current complexities of the fast-changing globalization society with prudence, ethics, and love.

The Seven Habits of Highly Effective People

Since the release of Stephen R. Covey's book 'The 7 Habits of Highly Effective People' in 1989, the book has become the definitive go-to source for the individual and organizational development literature. In this ground-breaking book, the author offers a practical and all-encompassing model of effectiveness that includes one's strengths, character, and principles in addition to performance results (Covey, 2004). It is, therefore, wrong to categorize the seven habits that Covey expounds as quick fixes, but they are deep paradigms that, when embraced, can cause a radical shift within one as well as between individuals (Ahmad et al., 2022). It is now fitting to go into each of these habits and discuss more as to why it is effective and how it can be used.

Habit 1: Be Proactive. The principle that is central to Covey's first habit is being proactive. Being proactive means understanding that one is the creator of one's life, and the decisions one makes together with one's outcomes are one's sole decisions and one's sole outcomes (Covey, 2004). This habit concerns effort on the things that are within people's control and not on the concerns that are not in their control. Proactive people do not complain but do not point at circumstances, situations, or the surroundings for their position state. Instead, they apprehend that they could fill in their patterns and responses towards any given contingency (Jarad et al., 2020). The advantage of perceiving health in such a manner is that it allows one to gain control from outside forces to inside forces. This is far from the truth, as by being proactive, one owns both the responsibility and authority to cause something to happen.

The following sum up the main activities that are involved in regulating this habit: self-awareness, self-initiation, and appropriate use of assertive language. A proactive person does not say 'I cannot' or 'If only'; they say things like 'I choose to' or 'Let me run through our options.' The language difference shows the difference between the victim mentality and the empowered mentality. The findings of Ahmad et al. (2022) reveal that people who show positive, proactive work behavior are likely to succeed both in their workplace and in their private lives. In addition, research conducted by Jarad et al. (2020) indicated a positive relationship exists between proactive personality and job performance as well as career advancement. When this habit is developed, one can easily deal with the challenges that life presents and find a way of unleashing the next level of success.

Habit 2: Begin with the End in Mind. The second of seven habits is interpersonal leadership, which encourages the observation of how people lead themselves and the need to ascertain their destination before setting out. This habit defines what one aims at with one's life and acts accordingly or refers to a plan for living. Beginning with the end in mind requires constructing the end in one's mind before constructing anything on paper. It is all about identifying the end goal one wants to attain in every aspect of life and then making an analysis of the things that are necessary to get there. The procedure helps one to keep their initiatives focused and coherent with the general goals every day. Covey (2004) gives his reasons for writing a personal mission statement as one of the ways of defining what one stands for. The statement can be viewed as a personal, detailed code of ethics that one can use to assess one's decisions and conduct. They offer purpose and goals, guiding a person through daily challenges and hurrying where needed by paying attention to the essentials. Williamson et al. (2022)meta-analysis of research in goal-setting theory found that both specific and difficult goals have superior performance to non-specific or non-difficult goals. Thus, the use of the ' starting with the end in mind' approach makes it possible to define realistic and well-grounded goals and objectives to encourage the efficiency of activities.

Habit 3: Put First Things First. The habit follows the previous two based on the proactive approach of self-management of one's own behavior. It relates to coordinating and planning work according to activities that are significant. Covey (2004) points out that it is necessary to differentiate between the urgent and the important and focus on tasks that help to achieve the desired goals and reflect one's values. The habit brings the time management matrix, which segregates tasks according to their importance and their urgency. The anchor for doing this is to spend most of one's time working on Quadrant II, activities that are important but not urgent. These would be predominantly planning, prevention, relationship building, and self-development tasks, which tremendously help one to be efficient but which people avoid due to their apparent insignificance compared to crisis management tasks. This means that the process of putting this habit into practice entails cultivating the ability to stay focused on significant work, even though it may not be urgent. It demands the ability to turn down less important and time-consuming activities and to control time properly. A calendar with schedules and to-do lists can be used, and, in fact, it is all about integrating this habit with one's values and personal or business objectives. Research conducted by Wilson et al. (2021) in the field of time management has identified that the level of stress can be reduced significantly if priorities are set rightly, which, as a result, enhances productivity. The research also suggested that students who effectively sorted out their priorities observed enhanced learning and decreased stress levels.

Habit 4: Think Win-Win. The fourth habit sets the organization and interpersonal leadership as the overall new focus of Covey's approach. According to Covey (2004),Think Win-Win is a way of thinking and approaching all dealings with other people that expects and looks for a parity of gain. It is all about struggling for success and thinking that the success of one team or one person does not deter the success of others and that there is enough success for everyone. The habit disapproves of the philosophy that the world operates in a way in which one just has to gain at the loss of another. It encourages the notion that conflicts can be resolved through innovative collaboration and people's appreciation and adherence to each other's rights. This is not about compromise, being polite, or appeasing anyone; it is about standing up for what one believes in. Formation of this habit can involve consideration, that is, empathy for others, and courage, which refers to assertiveness. They range from effective communication to successful conflict-solving and the ability to respect others' points of view. Thinking win-win is useful when it comes to negotiations and conflict-solving processes because it opens better and more effective ways to win. In negotiation and conflict management, studies show the positive outcome of thinking win-win. A study conducted by Bush (2020) revealed that the negotiators who followed the win-win approach were able to gain higher results and better satisfying agreements than those who considered the negotiation as a competitive battle.

Habit 5: Seek First to Understand, Then to Be Understood. The fifth habit relates to empathy in communication practices, where leaders seek to listen and understand others. The act of listening, as highlighted in the text, incorporates paying attention in a way that demonstrates the desire to comprehend the speaker. This habit is to build the practice of empathetic listening, that is, listening with the ears, mind, and heart to the essence and feelings behind words. In this perspective, Covey (2004) affirms that the majority of people listen autobiographically; that is, they listen with biases, predispositions, and reference points. Empathic listening, on the other hand, entails the act of temporarily suspending one's own model and focusing only on the speaker's view. This way, it is possible to establish better relationships with others while also problem-solving and avoiding conflicts within the relationships. The cultivation of this change requires time, willingness, and the ability to put aside one's prejudices. It includes questions that enable one to understand further what was meant, summarizing what one has comprehended not only on a content level but also on a feeling and purpose level. Communication literature has, for example, highlighted the value of empathic listening time and again. Research conducted by Andolina and Conklin (2021) established that people who engaged in empathic listening were among the most effective in helping fellow human beings solve issues, as they were seen as more supportive.

Habit 6: Synergize. The sixth habit is related to creative collaboration. According to Covey (2004), synergy isdefined as the phenomenon wherein the overall effect of two or more things is superior to the individual effects of the said things. It must be about appreciating diversity and joining divergent views to generate new choices and options. Synergy simply refers to the kind of combination where diverse people come together and, in an environment characterized by honesty, arrive at better solutions than if every part had tried for a solution on its own. It is centered on how one can use talents and perceive differently to maximize excellent performance. Applying this habit is characterized by creating a culture of trust and surrounding rationale for change. It presupposes the capacity to appreciate and use the diversity of approach, knowledge, and talent. Synergy is usually identified during the idea-generation meetings as well as merging times to tackle issues together. The studies in the field of teams and innovations confirm that synergy works. The study conducted by Huang et al. (2022) illustrated that groups composed of individuals possessing dissimilar backgrounds and abilities and being properly coordinated excel at solving intricate challenges as compared to identical groups.

Habit 7: Sharpen the Saw. The last habit is about continuous improvement and renewal. In 'Sharpen the Saw,' this means active sustaining and building of one's most valuable resource—oneself. According to Covey (2004), it is about regularly renewing oneself in the four basic dimensions of life: physical abuse, social and emotional abuse, neglect that may be physical, mental, or both, and spiritual abuse. Physical renewal is the proper nourishment, exercise, and rest of the body. Social or emotional renewal means obtaining the appropriate connection and performing the proper care of other people. Mental renewal means activities such as reading, writing, or practicing something new. It is important for one to get some rest; spiritual renewal is when one gets in touch with one's beliefs or prays or sits in nature. The habit that has to be developed is personal professionalism, which implies caring for oneself and learning continually. It means dedicating a particular period of time to those activities that restore individuals' physical, emotional, intellectual, social, and spiritual energies. Such a balanced transition is critical for sustaining its efficiency and, at the same time, preventing the professionals from getting too exhausted. The findings in different disciplines agree with the centrality of self-care and lifelong learning; for instance, a study by Gonçalves et al. (2022) revealed that workers with a higher frequency of self-care practices are likely to be satisfied with their jobs and experience less burnout.

Integrating the Seven Habits. Although each habit is great by itself, change is most effective when all seven habits are implemented as a system for managing life and leading others. These habits come in sequences; habits one to three are dependent on the previous because habit one lays the foundation for habit two, and so on, until they get to interdependent habits four to six, with habit seven as a repeating cycle to keep self-improvement (Covey, 2004). The first three habits, on the other hand, address personalization, which prepares an individual from a dependence stage to an independence stage. They are a set of principles originating from assertiveness that encompass accepting the responsibility of one's life, determining what gives values, and maneuvering one's life activities in accordance with the determined value systems (Ahmad et al., 2022). The next three habits are related to work in interactions with other people, transitioning from individual work to interdependent work. They make sure that all the other habits are maintained through their renewed and improved versions all the time.

Challenges in Implementing the Seven Habits. Although the principles of the seven habits are very useful, there are often challenges in implementing them. One of these challenges is resistance to change; for instance, changing habits usually comes with the need to eradicate past habits that are not useful, and this might be a challenge. Another problem is short-term orientalization because people are too busy with their existence to concentrate on personality growth (Covey, 2004). However, there are some challenges related to self-reflectiveness, and some people may fail to perform introspection, which is essential to practicing the said habits (Ahmad et al., 2022). Environmental characteristics are also difficult, and unfavorable environments at other centers or homes can lead to the consistent neglect of these habits. Tackling these realities entails dedication, time, and effort, as well as assistance from other people.

Conclusion: Stephen Covey's Seven Habits of Highly Effective People can be regarded as a holistic approach to personal and professional transformation. By focusing on principles of effectiveness rather than quick-fix techniques, this approach provides a sustainable path to growth and success (Covey, 2004). These habits provide a framework for taking responsibility in people's lives to the constant renewal of self to provide a more ethical and meaningful blueprint of how people can be more than just efficient workers but better moral beings as well (Ahmad et al., 2022). Thus, it is the practical value of the knowledge presented in the book, along with seven habits, that people can see when they are struggling through the labyrinth of the contemporary world.

How Each Habit should be used to develop the Community or to build People around You

Habit 1: Be Proactive. On a community level, being proactive involves taking the first steps to fix problems and bring about change without waiting for other people to do so. When done collectively, this habit can be a powerful tool used to enhance community development. To use this habit in building up others and developing the community, it is necessary to foster the culture of taking initiative and accepting responsibilities. According to the Haitian social context, being proactive is to engage people to play a role in tackling issues that affect the community. To increase the level of Haitians' involvement in community needs assessment, solution development, and self-organizing. It empowers people, boosts esteem, and encourages locally driven progress, which is crucial due to Haiti's socio-economic context. These groups can decide to target areas that need to be developed, such as the environment, young people, or businesses within the community. What it does mean is that one empowers people to take an active role in making the community a better one and gives them a focus to direct their efforts in a productive manner. The final area of proactivity is the ability to foresee possible difficulties in the future and adapt to them (Covey, 2004). This could include periodic surveys within the community to determine emerging concerns that may develop into significant problems. An example from the Bible is when Nehemiah demonstrated a proactive attitude when he learned about the condition of the Jerusalem walls (King James Version, 2019). Rather than just complain, he acted, prayed, and went to King Artaxerxes to seek permission to rebuild. His leadership ensured that the community worked towards rebuilding the protection of their city. Education is a key factor that can help promote proactivity. Seminars and workshops, for instance, on community leadership, problem-solving, and project development, can enable an individual to be ready to take charge.

Habit 2: Begin with the End in Mind. The second habit applied in the process of community development entails the emergence of a vision towards the future. This process of collective visioning can be wonderful in pulling a group together and mobilizing resources. To apply this habit, suggest introducing community visioning forums at which representatives from various spheres of a community's life voice their visions for a better future (Covey, 2004). Applying this habit in Haiti's community-centered culture entails thinking about the advancement of the community. Leaders should involve locals in identifying common goals and objectives that ensure they embrace Haitian culture and beliefs. It is unifying, enabling, and prescriptive, as it focuses on realizing the best of what is possible by countering adversity with assets of the community. The ultimate aim is to come up with a vision that is in accordance with the vision of the entire society (Jarad et al., 2020). An illustration from the Bible is the case whereby Jesus Christ started his ministry with a vision as described in Luke 4:18-19 (King James Version, 2019). He understood that his ultimate purpose was to achieve the task of the prophet Isaiah, reminding people about the good news and liberation. This vision was evident in His actions and in the teachings that he shared with the people during His ministry.

Habit 3: Put First Things First. The third habit when applying to community development entails proper prioritization of the community and its projects as well as the available resources. This becomes a helpful habit to guarantee that community activities are being channeled in the right direction and that value is being delivered. In order to adopt this habit, one should initially create a system within the community dealing with the assessment and selection of projects and activities. One possibility is to develop a community priority committee that will be composed of stakeholders originating from various sectors of the community (Covey, 2004). When it comes to applying Habit 3 in the Haitian community-involved culture, it is possible to speak about remarkable changes. Value initiatives that have a target to increase family cohesion and community. The emphasis should be placed on partnerships on particular initiatives. Most often, these initiatives are based on the current local challenges related to education or health care, for example. Stress on the group's work on goals and time, including its members' interests, for the further progression and changes in the community's outcomes and powers (Jarad et al., 2020). This might be annual or biannual sessions that involve relevant community opinion in evaluating the progress, analysis of new problems or issues, and re-strategization (Ahmad et al., 2022). An example in the Bible is illustrated in Acts 6:1–7, where the apostles could not combine their evangelism and balancing accounts responsibilities (King James Version, 2019). They chose the deacons to take care of the necessary physical necessities of the food distributions so the assembled brethren could concentrate on prayers and the instruction of the Word—establishing priorities in their leadership.

Habit 4: Think Win-Win. The fourth habit, when incorporated into the area of community development, creates conditions that are more effective in terms of cooperation and win-win interaction (Covey, 2004). Solomon is a biblical example proving thinking-win-win with his wise judgment in 1 Kings 3:16-28 (King James Version, 2019). When two women came forward with the same baby, it showed who the real mother was, but at the same time, it did not embarrass either of them. The judgment also served to strengthen the community's confidence in his leadership. A good approach to the problem is in the framework of community mediation programs. This means that some of these programs can offer organizational structures that help to handle various conflicts concerning the community and come up with the best solutions. If people in the community are trained on how to mediate, they are likely to have a pool of people who can assist in the facilitation of the difficult processes of dialogue and bargaining. Another process is the formation of partnership programs, which can overlook the various sectors existing in the community. For instance, an initiative that connects local businesses to schools for internships and mentorship can foster situations where all the parties involved benefit; the business organizations get access to talent and new ideas, while the students receive practical experience along with directions in their occupations (Ahmad et al., 2022). When it comes to the concept of win-win in the context of community planning and development projects, finding multiple aims and objectives within a singular approach or action plan shall be considered a primary goal (Jarad et al., 2020). For instance, a project involving establishing a community garden may lead to the solution of problems of food insecurity and blight, as well as improve aesthetics and social cohesiveness. Through them, it is possible to identify how various community activities can complement each other for a higher effect. Thus, the win-win solutions should also be promoted and advertised because the concept of this approach should be reinforced. Use the community media platforms and forward successes made through the collaborations and how they impacted many players in society.

Habit 5: Seek First to Understand, Then to Be Understood. When engaging in the practice of the fifth habit in relation to community development, there is a need to emphasize people's ability and willingness to listen. The habit is helpful in fostering trust, particularly when it comes to conflict solving and when it comes to the decisions made by the community, which depend on the understanding of various individuals' points of view (Covey, 2004). A scriptural example is observed in John 4, where Jesus, being tempted to disregard the cultural prohibition of speaking with an alien woman, conversed with the Samaritan woman at the well (King James Version, 2019). He paid attention to her, knew her condition, and then preached to her the word of God. Such a strategy brought her change and affected the entire village of people around her. The main objective that should be stressed is the listening skills of the participants, making sure that before they start thinking about the solutions, they actualize what the other participant said and make sure they fully understand it. Increasing empathy that is obtained through recognition and appreciation of the emotions of others by training the heads of communities and the members of the communities will dramatically improve the quality of community interactions (Ahmad et al., 2022). Training sessions on active listening, non-aggressive communication, and cultural competence make it possible for people to embrace new ways of conflict-solving. Ideally, these skills are important for anybody with leadership power, for instance, local government employees, community organizers, and business people. Another significant factor that needs to be considered when putting into practice this habit is the accommodation of diversity, which calls for the provision of platforms for minorities to express themselves (Jarad et al., 2020). This might entail developing specific channels or focus groups through which such people feel at ease sharing their special issues and requirements.

Habit 6: Synergize. The sixth habit involves the use of the talents and assets of multiple people to arrive at a commonly desirable result that cannot be obtained individually. This habit focuses on making the community environment accepting of differences and actively looking for them because the presence of these differences leads to new ideas and solutions (Covey, 2004). One can see the New Testament example in the early church in Acts 2:42–47 working in synergy efficiently(King James Version, 2019). They pooled their resources, ate together, prayed, and encouraged each other. Due to this, growth was rapid, and the team offered a solid and coherent community that, in turn, attracted others. For instance, in the task force that would address homelessness, there could be social workers, real estate developers, healthcare givers, ex-homeless people, and merchants (Ahmad et al., 2022). Thus, if one compiles this number of facets together, one is likely to get more extensive and innovative solutions than what a number of groups with restricted outlooks can come up with. Another form of synergy can be the hackathons in the communities or, for instance, innovation challenges. Others consist of uniquely organized small-scale meetings that involve intensive face-to-face work and the participation of people with different skills from the community to address particular issues affecting the community. Thus, these events can allow for a new approach to solving problems and the overlapping of brain streams, which can contribute to escalating solutions and the development of innovation and an out-of-the-box thinking culture (Jarad et al., 2020).

Habit 7: Sharpen the Saw. The last of the habits, when used in the context of community development, relates to the sustainable enhancement of the community resources and their capabilities. This habit is important so that community initiatives remain sustainable and effective in the long run (Covey, 2004). An example from the Bible is in Luke 5:16, in which Jesus used to seclude Himself to pray and have spiritual strength (King James Version, 2019). The practice of getting refilled all the time is in line with his message of trying to balance his work and the mission to reach out to his disciples and whole communities. This way, guaranteeing a constant improvement of skills and knowledge within the community ensures that the social structure is much more robust (Ahmad et al., 2022). Another form of sharpening the saw is through routine health checks of the community. Such assessments should consider the social, economic, environmental, and personal dimensions of community welfare. In this way, it is possible to determine which areas of development the community is lagging behind in and modify the efforts accordingly (Jarad et al., 2020). Paying for community assets, as well as investing in community spaces, is another key facet of this habit. This might require periodic maintenance and enhancements to parks, recreation centers, and other public facilities.

CHAPTER 3

How to be an Effective Leader in Your Community?

Community leadership is a very big responsibility and involves power, communication, kindness, and knowledge, among others. For a person to act as a leader in their community there is a need to examine the scriptural principles of leadership and how they fit in contemporary communities. The Old Testament offers numerous examples of charismatic leaders, starting from Moses leading the Israelites in the desert and up to Jesus Christ (Wilson, 2020). These biblical characters portray aspects of character that current community leaders should seek to embody. The first of these qualities is servant leadership. The role of a community leader is not to be a boss but a servant, and only a competent one at that. Similarly, when Jesus was teaching his disciples, he said that it is not right to be great and be served, but one must be a servant to others (King James Version, 2019). Any leader of a community should follow this principle as a guiding tenet. This means that the decision-makers must be ready to sacrifice their own personal interests for the benefit of others in the community.

Another essential characteristic that is required in community leadership is integrity. Honesty is another virtue often stressed in the book of Proverbs, as well as ethical conduct. Any leader without character will not retain the respect and confidence of society for a long time. Thus, a community leader should be a man of integrity and honesty and should always act in the right and ethical manner, even in their personal life. It is also important to have wisdom and good judgment in order to be an effective leader in a community. According to the Bible, wisdom is a godly virtue that can only be attained through practice, thinking, and consulting (King James Version, 2019). A good leader understands that leadership involves both opening one's mouth and keeping silent, as well as the time to make a move and the time to wait (Wilson, 2020). They are also able to look at the wider picture and appreciate the implications of some decisions and actions.

Courage and resilience have been recognized to be important attributes of a community leader. It must be noted that on occasion, the leader has to encounter some problem, some opposition, or some form of failure. As reiterated to Joshua, a modern community leader is also encouraged to remain strong and courageous as he leads people to the preferred destination, which in this case is the Promised Land (King James Version, 2019). The courage should be based on faith and conviction, not on arrogance or stubbornness. However, compassion and empathy are the other factors that should be observed by a community leader. Additionally, empathy, which is the ability of the leader to be able to see the same things as the feeling of another person or the experience of identifying with and partly putting oneself in another's place, allows the leader to be much closer to their community. Jesus was compassionate; he was healing the sick, feeding the hungry, and consoling those who were sad. Likewise, a community leader should have strong sensitivity toward the people in the community as well as the issues that affect every member of the community (Wilson, 2020). The ability to convey information and interact with other people is essential for leadership roles, and this is more so in communities. This type of leadership currently requires someone who is able to communicate clearly a vision, mobilize people for action, and ensure that everyone in the community is free to speak the truth (Miner & Bickerton, 2020). They should be effective in oral communication, which involves the use of words both in speaking and listening, in order to avoid marginalization of any person within the community.

Another occupation attribute that is crucial in a community leader is lifelong learning. What can be seen is that the world is dynamic, and hence, communities are confronted with issues and vicissitudes all the time during the course of their development. These are the leaders willing to learn, seek knowledge, and change strategies when the time calls for it, which means successful leadership in these distinct years. Holistically, partnership and teamwork are other valuable competencies that will help to lead a community (Miner & Bickerton, 2020). Anyone who thinks that on their own, they can achieve everything is not a leader but a yes-man or a yes-woman. Implementers, once again, are similar to Nehemiah, who encouraged the people of Jerusalem to rebuild the walls of the city (King James Version, 2019). This involves the acceptance of the strengths and abilities of others, the assignment and coordination of tasks within the community, and the protection of the interests of the community.

The key differentiator between a good leader and a bad one is that a good leader is patient and persistent. Community change is a slow process, and leaders need to be willing to work for years. Noah, before the Lord sent him the flood, spent several years constructing the ark and proved that vision demands the caller to persevere even when they cannot see the outcome (King James Version, 2019). A good community leader must also provide good stewardship. In performing this stewardship, the following is expected: This entails the proper use of resources, be it financial, physical, or people power resources, for the achievement of positive objectives. The use of the literary work: The parable of the talents supports the topic by explaining how talents should be used profitably and increased as per one's abilities (Wilson, 2020). In a community context, this refers to thoughtful choices of the time, money, and energy one wishes to devote to pursuing the several goals of that community. Since humility is a core value that contributes towards the achievement of most of the other values of leadership, it is worth elaborating on it briefly. A humble leader also means that a leader understands his weaknesses and is ready for the people's criticism and judgment, as well as ready to admit his errors (Miner & Bickerton, 2020). These people know that management is not about the glory but about lifting people up. Finally, an ideal community leader should be able to define the direction and goals to be accomplished in society. It should help them to drill into the heads of the people a new vision of the future of their society. Such a vision should be built upon the scriptural values of fairness, kindness, and respect for every person. This vision has to be present with the leader, and furthermore, the leader has to be able to sell this vision and make people accept it and struggle for it.

For one to be a good leader in the Haitian community, it is important that the leader possess integrity, especially in the aspect of culture and pledge. In a way, it shows the community that one possesses the wisdom to combine traditional approaches with modern ones (Miner & Bickerton, 2020). A leader should also be bold in speaking on contentious issues such as poverty eradication, quality health care, and exercise tolerance, bearing in mind the difficulties the community is going through (Wilson, 2020). An effective leader should promote the culture of learning and enhance the learning of skills among the people in society.

How do you get involved in The Community?

Engaging in one's community is a very important part of Christians' lives because Biblical teachings call for everyone to love their neighbors. Engagement in community work not only has a positive impact on those nearby but also adds value to the life of the person volunteering. What it really needs is its people's active participation, time, effort, and resources in any form, shape, and size—a clear manifestation of Gospel values of service, charity, and stewardship (Wilson, 2020). In any case, one of the initial measures to become active in the community is to raise awareness about the local demand and supply. This means engaging oneself to sometimes watch and listen to what is happening in the neighborhood, town, or city. The religious texts recommend followers to be listeners to the needs of others, and listening is the beginning of being active in the community (Miner & Bickerton, 2020). Community members can read newspapers and journals to get first-hand information, go to local meetings, or have words with close neighbors in order to have first-hand experience of the problems people are facing in a particular region.

Volunteering can be described as one of the direct and effective approaches to being involved in the community. Such local and international non-profit organizations are very many and have increased over time, with issues touching on food banks, the homeless, education, environments, and many more. Volunteering, in other words, is enjoined upon Christians since the Bible has time and again prodded people to serve (Wilson, 2020). People can search for work that can be done on their own according to their abilities, preferences, and schedule. Any spare time that an individual can give, even volunteering for a few hours a month, can greatly impact the lives of other people and the well-being of society. Voting is another significant way in which people should engage themselves in local government and civil activities. This could involve watching town hall-style debates, participating in local elections, or even joining the local elections himself. Christians, especially the Protestants, were complying with the principle that the Bible encouraged individuals to be law-abiding citizens, and there was nothing wrong with becoming active participants in the local government (Miner & Bickerton, 2020). Therefore, knowing the events or discussions that are going on in the local areas and being engaged in the decision-making process assists in good governance of human affairs for the common good of society.

One aspect that people often ignore is that purchasing products from local businesses and participating in local programs is what counts as community involvement. Faithfulness is a key virtue that the Bible endorses as commanding stewardship of resources that pertains to businesses and should, therefore, be used positively to transform the economy of the community (King James Version, 2019). This can be shopping from the local stores, ordering meals from local restaurants, or getting services from local professionals. In turn, everyone contributes towards the development of the local economy, and the welfare of everyone in the society is enhanced. Doing other projects for society is also a very good way of participating in community services. In most societies, people collaborate to carry out cleaning activities, landscaping activities, or other tasks meant to enhance the region's sanitation (Karim et al., 2022). In addition to beautifying the area, such projects contribute to developing a feeling of pride in the community and encouraging the inhabitants' active participation. Biblically, it is required that people preserve the creation, and these activities can be seen as ways of honoring this portion of scripture.

It is advisable to participate in a community group that already exists or, better, start one because community/group efforts have the potential to achieve greatness. This could be a watch-warden group, a reading club, a sporting team, or a church or mosque association. Another area that the Bible stresses is sharing and cooperation, and this is well instilled by the functioning of the community groups (King James Version, 2019). These groups can thus be used as points of change in certain needs or interests within the community. Guiding is a sure way of building a better future for such a society. Skill, knowledge, and experience passed from one generation to another enable people to contribute to the development of the young generation and thus influence leaders of future generations (Karim et al., 2022). Mentorship is well illustrated in scripture, starting with Eli and Samuel and Paul and his follower Timothy. Schools, youth organizations, or local communities can offer a strong base for such groups, and the results of mentoring reflect not only the changes in the learner but also the mentor.

Participating in or organizing community events is another way to get involved. This could encompass cultural activities such as festivals, charity activities such as marathons, or any occasion festivities like holidays. Such functions create social cohesion as they gather folks together, and in most cases, they create awareness or ask for support for a cause. The scriptures teach believers to rejoice and assemble themselves together, and that is what community events offer (Wilson, 2020). Promoting significant issues is one of the methods that people need to indulge in to ensure a positive impact on society (Karim et al., 2022). Some of the advocacy measures could be writing letters of concern to some officials in the locality, addressing public assemblies, or conducting awareness creation. Through the scriptures, people of faith are encouraged to do justice and to speak for those who have no one to speak on their behalf. Thus, through supporting causes that are aligned with Bible standards, people can transform the world.

Charitable giving to local organizations and specific causes makes a real difference in the community. Of course, people might be asked or willing to give financial support and gifts, but donations may be physical or even in-kind. Giving is a major biblically supported notion that should be practiced in daily life, and helping local charities is one of the ways of doing so. It is evident that as little as they may be, each amount will go a long way in supplementing the gesture that other members of the same community are willing to extend (Wilson, 2020). Another way is to volunteer one's professional skills, which will be suitable for those people who have a certain amount of experience or certain knowledge in their field. This may entail representing non-profit organizations in court, offering medical treatment at a charitable health facility, or assisting small businesses with a financial task. The Scriptures teach that Christians should apply the talents that have been given to them to bless other people, and providing professional services free of charge is one way to accomplish this (Karim et al., 2022). They can use such interactions to understand each other's religions or cultures, hence combating hatred that may prevail within inter-dominating cultures. The dialogues also reveal contemporary attitudes toward neighbors and representatives of different faiths, following the Biblical command to love one's neighbor and the emphasis on the pursuit of peace. These engagements may result in an improvement in the unity and cooperation within the community.

Engagement in local schools is essential for anyone with a notion of wishing to make a positive impact on the people within the community. This could include going to class sections to help teachers, joining the Parent-Teacher Association, or being involved with extracurricular activities. The biblical value of education and the young are practices that the church cherishes, and engaging in local schools is among the practical ways of putting into practice these beliefs (King James Version, 2019). Last but not least, one can participate as a good neighbor, which is perhaps the most basic form of participation in the life of a community. This involves being friendly to those neighbors as well as being ready to assist them and not being a nuisance to them. It could mean ensuring elderly neighbors are reached, lawn mowing, or even inviting neighbors to a block party. In many ways, the biblical mandate to love one's neighbor is most arguably realized in these mundane practices of benevolence and togetherness. The Scriptures provided clear-cut revelations to support involvement in one's communities beyond just being a fulfilling process. It enables people to go about their beliefs and practice what they have learned in the Bible, giving them the ability to make change in society positively and improve the lives of other people in society (Wilson, 2020). Knowledgeable volunteers, citizens joining local governments, supporting initiatives, community service, joining groups, mentoring, event organization, lobbying for certain causes and needs, donating, offering skills, participating in discussion and dialogue, supporting schools, being a good neighbor, etc. can become valuable members and stakeholders in society

(Karim et al., 2022). These actions based on the principles of love, service, and stewardship derived from the Bible transform not only the community but also the people of the community engaging in them.

Role in Community as a Leader

Leadership in the community can be defined as a concept that has various and significant roles and is grounded in the Holy Bible. A community leader is a role model, an enabler, as well as a change agent and a decision-maker who displays the virtues of the so-called servants' leadership stemming from Jesus Christ (Karim et al., 2022). These duties and tasks are, in a way, social and developmental in nature, and all are predicated on the general improvement of society. Before all, a member of a community is a servant. This very aspect of leadership is well demonstrated throughout the scriptures, with Jesus Christ being an example of the leader who washed the disciples' feet. In the case of serving in a community, it means that one's focus is to work for the community's interest, as opposed to working for profit (King James Version, 2019). It entails the commitment of time and effort to work on issues pertaining to society to foster progress. This service-dominant logic is expected to infuse the leader's responsibilities, including decision-making processes, communication with other members of the community, and practices of leadership.

A big responsibility that is expected of a community leader is to be a visionary. Like the leaders who are chosen to lead the people of Israel in the Old Testament, modern leaders should possess this attribute to be effective in offering direction (Karim et al., 2022). This encompasses ascertaining a desired end vision, the ability to predict the future, and a preparation for how to work systematically to achieve a desired end vision. This needs to be communicated by the leader in such a manner that it creates the appropriate awareness to facilitate the achievement of managerial goals. This visionary aspect of leadership is very critical in offering direction and meaning during the stages of disaster. The leadership of a community also involves relationship management, of which the following are some of the sub-topics. The Holy Scripture puts much emphasis on togetherness and relationships, and a member of the community has a significant role in establishing such relations (King James Version, 2019). This ranges from contacting different groups of society and reconciling them to fostering discussion and partnership. A leader in the given community ought to ensure that they are reachable and friendly in order to make all the community members feel important, and whenever they are faced with issues, they should be able to easily report to the leaders (Wilson, 2020). It also applies to the development of networks with other legal entities and communities capable of positively impacting the community's development.

The community leader also works as a negotiator and a conflict solver. It is essential to note that conflict and any type of challenge arise in any community, and a leader is supposed to solve or manage such problems. This requires wisdom, patience, and, most importantly, discernment, which are core values in biblical leadership (Wilson, 2020). The leader should also be able to listen to different opinions, actively encourage a discussion, and seek a way forward. Sometimes, the leader has to overrule his subordinates and do what is best for the community, including being fair and square. Another important responsibility of a community leader is advocating. This includes voicing the needs and demands of the public, especially those who cannot or do not have the ability to do so. The Bible also warns of justice and the need to eschew the mistreatment of the vulnerable in the community, and a leader should follow this when advocating (King James Version, 2019). This might entail lobbying the higher authorities to provide the community with necessary funds, equipment, and material support or educational campaigns about issues affecting the community.

Education and empowering the people are also as important a part of being a leader in the community as protecting the common populace. Even though a leader is the head of a community or organization, they should perform as a teacher or an advisor who transfers knowledge and skills, as well as fosters leadership qualities across the community (Lansing et al., 2023). This encompasses providing a chance to learn at work and also gaining new skills, starting from a workplace trainer and a trainee relationship to a staff development program. Through facilitating others, a leader enlarges what they are able to do and contributes to the longevity of different community endeavors. A community leader also has an important function in the allocation of resources to their management, which includes the efficient use of such resources to yield maximum benefit (Jones, 2022). Bible education bears a message about stewardship; hence, this principle applies to community leaders. Managers are usually responsible for the administration of the community resources, which comprise financial, physical, and human resources. Their function is to safeguard and promote proper use and utilization of all these commodities and resources to create value for the mass populace. This includes decision-making in relation to the use of resources, honesty in financial management, and being able to answer questions from the community or people about how the resources will be used.

Another key responsibility of a community leader is to further innovation and adaptation in their given community. Things are always changing in communities, and new challenges or new opportunities are always likely to surface, hence the need for leaders to be in place to steer the communities (Lansing et al., 2023). This includes facilitating innovative thinking by embracing new solutions, embracing change, and appropriate ways of supporting the community. The leader ought to establish an atmosphere that encourages people to produce ideas constantly and to be prepared to implement changes when the previous strategies are futile. Additionally, the leaders of the communities act as role models. Paul's text is filled with epigrams that promote leadership by example; this was insisted on, especially at the community level

(King James Version, 2019). As a leader it should be noted that people tend to imitate the attitudes and actions of their leaders. This involves behavior in organizations and at work, such as adherence to professional standards, concern, perseverance, and professionalism in learning and development. Thus, leaders become role models, requiring others to work on the same level as required by society, with the ability to perform to the best of their capacity.

A key role of community leaders is to promote unity and inclusion. Christians believe that everyone is sinful and lost but has been created in the image of God and, therefore, is of immense worth (King James Version, 2019). People in the community should refrain from discriminating against others based on factors like color, religion, or their status in society. This encompasses a process of seeking change with regard to discriminating factors as well as fighting for marginalized groups to be given an opportunity to participate in a community decision-making process. The other key change participants and stakeholders in the crisis management process are the community leaders. In the social setting, any calamity or other situations that pose a threat to the population's safety turn to the leaders for direction, support, and quick action (Lansing et al.,

2023). It means that leaders always need to be ready for immediate response, for mobilization of all the means available, for good communication, and for being a steady source of orientation for the people after the disaster. This entails audacity, self-possession, and the capacity to make effective decisions in executing the obligations.

Another key responsibility that a community leader has is to foster a sense of community identity and pride. This entails promoting the social heritage of the society, culture, and success stories, as well as developing events that foster social relatedness. Leaders can arrange the events, including traditional ones, and promote local successes that will likely create a positive image of the community. Community leaders must ensure that they are held responsible for their actions. In order to establish contact with Haitian people, it is necessary to join different meetings and events related to Haitian culture, such as carnivals or religious holidays. Contribute services to non-profit organizations working on critical social causes in the community, such as education or health (Lansing et al., 2023). It is also good to learn Haitian Creole so as to be fluent enough to communicate with the people of Haiti (Charles, 2020). Additionally, arrange for common social groups to work on whole community strengthening projects such as Haitian music, which is a source of pride due to the diverse Haitian rhythms, Haitian paintings, and delicious Haitian foods (Charles, 2020). One should also actively participate in all activities regarding the particular culture while also ensuring that they always respect the culture of the respective area in which they are carrying out their development agendas.

How to Rise and Shine in the Community?

The act of rising and shining in one's community can be one that takes a great deal of effort, time, and a personal conviction to want to make a change or difference. It is not only for one to transform but also for one to transform others as well. The idea of rising and shining in a community overlaps with the biblical concept of being a light in the world and living one's purpose out in the world. To be up and about in a community, one needs to have a good support base within themselves (Karim et al., 2022). This starts with a clear understanding of mission and vision and a set of organizational values that are grounded in the Bible (King James Version, 2019). This is because anyone who wishes to be seen as a positive figure in their community should cultivate virtues like integrity, compassion, and humility, among others. These values, considered appropriate in religious texts, are the foundation of an individual's personality and determine his relations with others and attitudes toward community participation.

Education and development are some of the factors that define the growth and development of a society. The Bible calls for Christians to increase in wisdom and knowledge, and this is most appropriate in the leadership of communities (King James Version, 2019). It is important for a person to continue learning to pursue knowledge and skills from college, training, and personal development. This continuous learning process develops personal skills as well as prepares the individual for the responsibility of serving and leading the community (Lansing et al., 2023). Effective and mutual communication skills should be fostered by anybody willing to rise and shine in society. Thus, skills of being able to express ideas coherently, listen effectively, and negotiate constructively are essential in the context of communities. Speaking and writing enable a person to convey his ideas, motivate other people, and get them together to solve significant problems. Additionally, communicating across different groups in the community is significant in overcoming barriers, an aspect of community leadership that the Bible encourages.

Initiating activities is another facet of promoting the spirit of rising and shining in a given community. Instead of expecting others to notice the deficits as well as the possible good things that are missing in society, an individual should seek them and take the initiative to bring about change. This could be a new community project initiation, event management, or even recommending solutions to emergent situations in society. The Scripture reveals precedents of people who could seize the opportunity and become active in positively contributing to their society (King James Version, 2019). The same approach can help one become a subject who is recognized and valued for leading positive change. Therefore, the development of social capital within the community is another strategy to adopt to rise and shine. This involves participating in regular interaction with the various stakeholders, right from the local authorities, the business community, volunteers, and inhabitants of the community in question (Lansing et al., 2023). It is essential to build real relationships and partner with people or organizations so that one's own efforts can have a powerful multiplier effect. The Bible also focuses on the aspects of unity and cooperation, and the above relationships comprise the core of community leadership.

In enhancing the spirit of a community to rise and shine, the use of words and positive actions should match. It has been observed that people pay attention to those who do what they promise to do and who walk the talk. It establishes reliability, which is critical when trying to foster change and be relevant to the society or people one is aiming for. Thus, one can refer to the biblical principle that he who is faithful in a little will be faithful in much—in other words, if, over time, one can be punctual, reliable, and competent in small matters, they will be considered for the major leadership responsibilities (King James Version, 2019). Achieving or excelling in one's work or any field as a profession is also a way to 'Rise and Shine' in a community. Regardless of the roles and responsibilities, whether one is working for pay or as a volunteer, one is associated with great results all the time. This should be accompanied by readiness and desire to do more than what is required, in compliance with the scriptural confession of doing just about everything to God (Karim et al., 2022). Whenever people see that an individual performs well and is willing to go above and beyond, they will be quick to follow the leader.

Acceptance of hardships and struggling to overcome crises is important for growth and rising and shining in a community. Stake postulates that there are always challenges in community work, and how a person copes with the challenges determines him/her as a leader. Electing to stand on faith, and per the illustration, it rises and occurs again after a fall as a way of encouraging others in the community (Wilson, 2020). Many examples can be found in the Bible with people who overcame sufferings and hardships in order to accomplish great things; in light of this, modern community leaders have examples to emulate (King James Version, 2019). Another way of differentiating is to offer something new to the community problems, coming up with new ways of solving them. That means, as the clown says, accepting the idea of inventiveness in approaching perennial issues and problems, suggesting new angles, and being able to take chances. As much as such leaders have to adhere to customs and conventions as well as institutional frameworks in place, an individual capable of bringing new solutions to problems that communities face tends to gain fame. This innovation has to be done with wisdom, as is stressed in the Bible, as new ideas must benefit society.

The act of mentoring and nurturing others is one of the most effective ways of rising and shining in a community. The possibility of positively influencing other people, especially the youths, and ensuring that they acquire certain skills and leadership qualities can, therefore, go a long way in achieving such a legacy. This can be uniquely compared to the discipleship process, where someone shares knowledge with other people for the generation of knowledge and wisdom (Wilson, 2020). Whenever one acts in the interest of other people and assists them in achieving their goals, they gain recognition among their counterparts. Another way of rising and shining is to speak for the things that need to be spoken for and stand up for helpless individuals. This calls for the use of one's voice or power to rectify wrongs within a society and to champion the causes of the marginalized in the society. Justice and judging are mentioned in the Bible as things that believers should pursue, including defending the helpless in community advocacy, which may enhance one's identity, status, and role immensely (King James Version, 2019).

Cultural competence is now a crucial aspect in organizations due to the rising diversity across the globe. Rising and shining involves the capacity to connect the gaps so as to foster a culture that will allow everybody in society to respect one another. This corresponds to the principles of love for the neighbor and acknowledgment of every person's equal value before God (King James Version, 2019). Applying technology intervention and social media and achieving one's full potential within the community can be possible. As long as one learns to balance the use of these tools, social media platforms and technology can be used as tools for reaching out to members of the community, passing information, and encouraging the mobilization of people for the right cause (Lansing et al., 2023). When such a person has learned how to deal with these tools in a proper manner as they keep building their actual and unique relationships, they are able to significantly expand the reach of their influence.

Thanking and acknowledging the efforts of the people around is one of the essential elements that are left unpracticed while motivating oneself to get up and work in a community. Praise for one another, the good achievements going around the community, and commendation for the work done not only raise the morale of the community but also bring honor to the praised individual and have him or her recognized (Lansing et al., 2023). Such an attitude is quite biblical in terms of practices concerning thanksgiving and good humility, as recommended by the scriptures (Wilson, 2020). Several things have to be understood by those individuals who would like to wake up one day and start shining in that society: One has to stay focused in a long-term manner. Often, it takes a long period to bring about real and sustainable change, and those who can stay loyal to their goals and beliefs during these processes contribute the most. This kind of devotion, which can be compared with biblical prophets who continued their work for years, led to the penetration of the culture into the community and the gaining of stable, permanent results.

How to Impact the Community

The act of contributing to the overall improvement of one's community is a worthy endeavor for Christians, which correlates strongly with advancing the gospel's message regarding service, love for a fellow man, and being good stewards of the gifts that have been given to them by the Lord (King James Version, 2019). Creating positive change is a process that requires a series of activities and the development of character traits, wherein the overriding goal is bringing about a salutary effect on other people. Thus, though there may be many specific procedures for an individual to influence the community, there are several general strategies and guidelines for the task. Volunteering is one of the most raw and direct ways of changing the community, as it actively involves giving back. Thus, the time and effort of local organizations, initiatives, or causes can help an individual contribute to the satisfaction of certain needs in the community. Examples of voluntary work could include volunteering at a food bank, helping young people, cleaning the environment, or helping the elderly (Lansing et al., 2023). The scripture provides for the proactively volunteering principle that one should serve others and that through volunteering, one is able to, for instance, change the fate of a fellow citizen.

The other significant intervention worthwhile to implement is to launch and coordinate community development projects. This includes recognizing existing gaps or areas of improvement within the community that were not met and then acting on them. It may be a simple case of starting a garden in a particular estate, developing a watch-band system within the estate, or having an organization for a certain group of people. When one takes such action, they not only solve a current problem but, at the same time, raise public awareness and motivate other people to help (Lansing et al., 2023). Another important reason is that sharing knowledge and skills is one of the most effective ways to change society or a given community. Every person has something to offer others, some form of knowledge or skill that may be of value to mankind (Karim et al., 2022). This could mean providing free training in bodybuilding, as well as freely giving advice in the capacity of specialists or simply giving tips to neighbors on how to perform exercises. The concept of stewardship also applies to one's knowledge and skills, which, when freely given, enable others and society in its entirety to grow.

Advocacy is another important way of impacting a community, and it involves being an advocate for good issues, administrative and social change, and policies and decisions of a community. It could involve participating in the Meet the People forum, sending letters to political leaders, or engaging in sensitization. The holy book, as a blueprint of Christianity, promotes justice and allows one to stand up for the voiceless, and thus, through advocacy, an individual can influence the course and agenda of a society (King James Version, 2019). Financial help can also possess a great influence on a community. Of course, not every person is able to donate thousands of dollars, but even small, regular contributions to local charities, community organizations, or the cause that is close to their heart matter (Lansing et al., 2023). This is based on giving, as stated in the Bible, and therefore, by wisely investing money in the community fields, one will be able to find important works to support and give a boost with the aim of benefiting many.

Creating social bonds and enhancing existing relationships in the community is a more obscure but no less powerful kind of change. This entails interacting with neighbors, taking part in community events, and making the neighbors feel that they are part of the community. People build up social capital that can be mobilized to solve problems, mark achievements, and build a stronger community. The Bible teaches about the significance of fellowshipping and being together as disciples, and if an individual invests in their relations, then they are part of building the social structure of the society (King James Version, 2019). Education and recourse to learning contribute to the improvement of a community, and these changes are long-lasting. This might, therefore, involve helping students, working with local schools, setting up book clubs, or helping create education-based awareness among adults. By nurturing a culture of learning and constantly developing one's intellect, one can help build society and bring about improvements that may be reaped in the distant future (Lansing et al., 2023). This explains why the biblical value pertaining to wisdom and understanding makes a lot of sense when it comes to formulating methods of influencing change in the community.

Environmental stewardship has become a popular way of contributing to society. Such can entail environmental conservation campaigns, recycling programs, or efforts aimed at cleaning up the environment within a certain community (Yuriev et al., 2020). It would cover activities like recycling collection campaigns, planting of trees, or even just explaining or raising awareness of any environmental problems that are around the environment. This type of community impact coincides with the biblical commandment to steward God's creation and positively influences the current and future generations (King James Version, 2019). Promoting the local economy and people's commercial activities is another way of contributing to some of these fields. This could include buying locally produced products, supporting local artists and business people, or joining the buy local produce schemes like those for food (Lansing et al., 2023). In their attempt to support a local business venture, an individual is playing a role in the creation of employment, stimulating sustainable economic development, and preserving the culture of the society.

    Civic activity is thus one major way of influencing a community. This pertains to the act of participating in local polls, making applications for board or committee membership, and familiarizing oneself with local matters. Democracy is, therefore, a process that any one person can engage in so as to influence decisions that affect all people. To lead a Christian life and be good stewards, Christianity supports people's active participation in political activities, which is a key element of civic activity (King James Version, 2019). Promoting the concept of diversity in society is another aspect that can make society a better place. It means engaging in efforts that make society address the divides, enhance the coexistence of the various factions, and guarantee every person's dignity (Lansing et al., 2023). It might mean arranging cultural fairs, promoting changes in accessibility regulation, or moderating discussions on difficult topics. The biblical source of understanding people as equals made in the image of God can be regarded as a very solid background for this work on people's unity in diversity.

One of the significant ways to influence the future of a society is through mentoring young people. It is always fulfilling when an individual spends their time and energy to guide, encourage, and support young people, and the result is the formation of society's future leaders and active citizens. They can also join a corporate or school-based program that includes mentoring young people and students, being athletic trainers for the school's sports teams, or being a simple role model for youth in need in the area. Thus, the Bible gives many examples of mentoring, stressing the significance of the transfer of knowledge and values (King James Version, 2019). Thus, to a large extent, the improvement of health-promoting strategies has a great impact on the quality of life of a community. This may mean getting in touch with one's physical self through joining a fitness class, educating peers on proper mental health, or even raising awareness on proper healthcare. Since taking care of members' physical and mental health contributes to health improvements and rates of activity, an individual fosters a healthier community (Lansing et al., 2023). This corresponds with the biblical teachings, as the body is a temple that needs to be taken care of, as well as taking care of fellow human beings.

Another plausible strategy focuses on applying professionally learned competency for the improvement of people's lives. Whether one is a lawyer willing to do legal aid, a carpenter who volunteers to do some renovation on an elder's home, or a marketing specialist helping non-profit organizations—bringing professional skills to the needs of a community can do a lot. Once again, this corresponds with the scripture's truth that man should use all his strengths and opportunities for the benefit of others (Karim et al., 2022). Promoting positivity in a society is one of the best ways of enriching the lives of people in that society or community (Lansing et al., 2023). This includes enacting and modeling exercises and examples of small kindness, encouraging consideration of others' feelings and tone, and the feeling of community within the center. It can also be done by scheduling a meal train for needy families, establishing the community kindness challenge, or just practicing kind acts in one's life. The concept of this approach is based on the biblical injunction of Christians, which inculcates the spirit of love for neighbors.

Another significant contribution is in maintaining and promoting the culture and history of a community. This could mean coordinating heritage activities, writing tapes, and advocating in a bid to conserve history. If one is to link the community to its origin and establish a cultural identity, then he plays a significant role in uniting the community against difficulties. This is in concordance with the word of God's emphasis on the need to remember one's roots and ancestry (King James Version, 2019). Finally, the demonstration of good character or ethical culture in one's life is very powerful to a society. When an individual in a society is proven to be a man of principle, caring and concerned for other people's welfare, and is concerned most especially in the improved welfare of the society, then such an act will serve as a catalyst for change to be cultivated in the society (Lansing et al., 2023). This leadership, though almost invisible, works hand in hand with the teachings of the Bible, where one is called to be a light in the darkness, and that character does matter.

Therefore, being able to create an impact within a community is so complex that it involves being intentional, persistent, and knowledgeable about the welfare of other people. Volunteerism, leadership, knowledge, advocacy, finances, networking, education, environment stewardship, economic support, citizenship, diversity, mentoring, health and promotion, professional services, generosity, cultures, and ethics counseling are some of the ways that one can bring change to any community (Lansing et al., 2023). The many forms of these activities based on genuinely Christian concepts of love, service, and stewardship do not just raise up the condition of the community but ennoble the person working for these improvements (King James Version, 2019). Sometimes, the mark one leaves on one's community shapes the existence of future generations by making progressive changes in society.

How to Engage the Community in Projects?

The involvement of the community in projects is a critical factor that defines the efficiency of community development and leadership. It guarantees that the developed plans are usable, feasible, and definite as shaped by various stakeholders. The community engagement process complies with the cult of the Bible since it compromises unity, cooperation, and recognition of each person's worth (Karim et al., 2022). Concerning goals and objectives, the trio reiterates that leaders have to ensure they lay down their vision when involving the community. This entails bringing out the positive gains and potential effects of the change that are culturally sensible to the people in the community (Anthony, 2023). The idea is to include a number of aspects and different directions of the community's development to respond to the needs of various community stakeholders.

Thus, offering great chances for relevant and real participation is a critical task. This can involve scheduling meetings of the public forums, such as town hall meetings, consciously creating specific focus groups, or even designing web interfaces for feedback and work ideas (Anthony, 2023). The idea is to ensure that there are many ways through which the whole community can share their ideas, issues, and recommendations. Thus, this concept of including all the people relates to the biblical principles of accepting everyone and the affection that lies in each of them that make up the 'body of Christ' (King James Version, 2019). It has also become clear that the development of relations with different organizations, businesses, and institutions of the community can greatly improve the situation. These partnerships can help someone obtain the resources as well as the expertise that is needed—an additional means to get in touch with the members of the community. Organizing with an existing structure shows respect for the existing organizational structures and takes advantage of relations already in place.

Engagement can be taken to more people through social media and the use of technology, as seen in the following. Opinion polls on the Internet, company websites, and social networking campaigns can attract youths and others who possibly cannot attend meetings. Nevertheless, one has to be always in touch and use certain face-to-face methods in order to reach all segments of the community (Anthony, 2023). Endowing the members of the community with certain facets of the project can also enhance their participation. This might involve then forming subcommittees and roles or promoting local participation in various aspects of the large project (Wallerstein et al., 2020). Individuals or a group of people will always ensure that the project succeeds when they feel that it belongs to them.

Consequently, the application of transparency and other practices in relation to the communication cycle is essential in the creation of engagement during the various phases of a project.

Updating the community, thanking them for their efforts, and sharing some issues enhance trust and people's participation (Wallerstein et al., 2020). The concept holds with the word of God, as it encourages one to be honest or accountable in all they do. It is equally important for members of a community to come together and fete the achievements made within that community. Acknowledging the team and individual achievement also creates and sustains motivation, thus enhancing the community feeling. These celebrations can also act as platforms through which the society can call back inactive members who may have reduced their participation in the society's activities (Anthony, 2023). Therefore, there are several tenets in managing projects that involve the community, namely: a culture of acceptance of diversity, participation, and partnership; the use of technology in an appropriate manner; the recognition of people's potential; public accountability; and valuing the successes made. By doing this, this approach not only guarantees the success and growth of projects, thus making them sustainable but also fosters the cohesiveness and development of the social setting of the community, thus impacting principles such as unity as recommended in the Bible.

CHAPTER 4

With increasing levels of globalization, persons and entities are endowed with the abilities and duty to affect the world locally and globally. This is a practical manual that looks into ten biblical paradigms of doing community development focusing on Haitians (Lowe, 2023). These approaches attempt to solve almost every concern with regard to community development, ranging from the spiritual or religious perspective, as well as economic empowerment and social justice (Salusky et al., 2020). If one wants to bring positive change to their local community or extend it to the less fortunate populations in other countries, then these concepts provide the blueprint of how it can be done.

1. Spiritual Outreach and Evangelism

Outreach and evangelism are the primary approaches to spreading the word of God as contained in the Bible to society, especially targeting Haitian society locally and in other parts of the world. This approach acknowledges the fact that change has to start somewhere and that this is in the spiritual realm where a person relates to the Supreme Being. In the case of Haitian populations, religiosity implies a different perspective because, in Haitian culture, this is closely related to spirituality, where there are strong roots in Christianity (Lowe, 2023); however, extended and intertwined with beliefs involving elements of Vodou or other related practices found in Haitian pop culture. Successful and efficient spiritual outreach operations that encompass organized Haitian communities work best by identifying the practicing youth as well as the other subgroups and setting up bible study sessions for them, depending on the level of their spiritual training (Salusky et al., 2020). These groups entail organizations that involve people, allow them to ask questions, and explain different aspects of the faith and bible. Attendees could be people who attend gospel concerts, outdoor crusades, and film festivals themed on faith.

Frequently, in Haiti itself, there might be a lack of resources that can help people develop their faith; therefore, donating Creole-language Bibles, study kits, and other kinds of Christian literature can play a significant role in supporting people's spiritual journeys. Regarding the second topic, cooperating with the local churches and ministries assists in guaranteeing that such materials get to those that require them and are relevant to the local culture (Miner & Bickerton, 2020). It may also be noted that this approach contributes to the encouragement of individual spiritual growth and enhances faith-based organizations at the local level. One of the facilitative steps in spiritual evangelism is to empower local people or leaders. In supporting Haitian pastors, evangelists, and lay leaders, spiritual outreach initiatives serve a multi-fold purpose. It could mean that churches have to offer events such as leadership seminars, funding scholarships for theological studies, or creating sponsorship whereby young ministers are benchmarked with seniors (Karim et al., 2022). Hence, it enables locals to organize and carry out spiritual interventions in the future after initial solutions have been provided.

Basically, when one is interested in conducting spiritual interventions in Haitian communities, one has to do so with adequate cultural sensitivity. This will require the use of time to study how Vodou fits some of the Haitian communities today and how one can share the gospel in harmony with culture while sticking to the truth of scripture (Lowe, 2023). It creates a rapport and provides an opportunity for further discipleship to take place in faith-related issues. In essence, spiritual evangelism or ministry among Haitian people calls for transpersonal intervention and resources that also condemn the sickness (Miner & Bickerton, 2020). This may entail linking evangelism with the relief work or provision of commodities like food, shelter, medicine, and education. Hence, by implementing this method of love through action, the hindrances to the gospel message can be removed, and the hearts of people can be prepared to accept the good news. This is a model of ministry according to the scriptures, where people are ministered to in the spirit and in the body.

Diaspora Haitian spiritual ministries may require solutions to tackle issues such as cultural assimilation, integration, and the general experience of living in a different society. Services that assist clients in retaining cultural and spiritual relationships since they are transplanted elsewhere could be especially useful (Karim et al., 2022). This may be serviced in Creole, religious holidays, and Christianity, mixed with cultural practices and groups for those who have recently arrived in America. Technology can be very useful in contemporary spiritual evangelism, and by engaging young people and those who do not fancy the traditional church setting, then the use of social media, online Bible study, and other online resourceful platforms can be of great benefit (Miner & Bickerton, 2020). Haitian society is gradually connected to the Internet, which allows digital outreach to strengthen printed initiatives or send information to inaccessible locations.

Other aspects of spiritual care that may be included in the practice of spiritual care in Haitian populations are education about faiths other than their own. However, staying a non-funded denomination with a clear focus on evangelism and witnessing does not hinder sharing the gospel with people of other religious beliefs and traditions. The approach entails some level of intelligence, time, and sheer consideration for the other person's view (Karim et al., 2022). Therefore, the target of spiritual evangelization in Haitian societies is to raise people's souls in their communities with regular interaction with God to change their lives, including their communities. In this way, such approaches can become an important addition to the overall development of the community with the help of presenting the message of hope and rescue through the Gospel, the solution of practical issues, and the consideration of cultural values (Lowe, 2023). Thus, the growth of a person in faith and biblical knowledge promotes the transformation of families, neighborhoods, and greater society, with a resulting ripple effect of spiritual and social change.

2. Education and Literacy Initiatives

The subject areas of education and literacy offer one of the most effective ways to empower Haitian communities, whether in Haiti or in the diaspora. These biblical activities understand the value of knowledge and want to break barriers, change people's lives, and positively impact society. One of the most tangible ways of helping influence education for the people of Haiti will be through supporting and creating institutions, more particularly, schools (Guzmán et al., 2020). This means it can include building new schools in those areas for children who have none, supporting good schools that need help with infrastructure and materials, or even giving money for the operating costs and teachers' wages (Kowalski et al., 2022). In the context of the Haitian education system, where numerous problems undermine the quality and children's access to education, such actions can be vital in providing basic education to children.

Nevertheless, in addition to concentrating on children's schooling since it is a population that directly profits from it, adult literacy also plays a crucial role in community development. Adult education can facilitate the instruction of classes specifically for Haitian people, and these classes can be taught in both Creole and French. Such programs can be of high effectiveness if used together with vocational preparedness or business learning, helping adults boost their financial position in addition to their literacy (Guzmán et al., 2020). In many cases, the lack of significant educational input affects the processes of obtaining knowledge in many regions of Haiti. This can be offset by Christian-based organizations by providing the needs of schools and other community-based education institutions, such as books and stationery, as well as other materials that are Bible-based. Additionally, bringing in technology in terms of instructional technology aids like tablets with teaching software or a computer lab connected to the internet can be used to share a way of closing the technology gap and preparing the students for the future (Kowalski et al., 2022). It is with respect to the quality of teachers that teaching and, consequently, the quality of education being offered are determined. Programs that address the concerns with teacher education and teacher training will go a long way in influencing educational achievements. This might include conducting training sessions for teachers on best practices, observing the new teachers, and offering them constant support or funding for higher learning in education.

Since Haiti and the Haitian communities around the world are blessed with diverse linguistic skills, it is appropriate for them to support bilingual education. Classes involving both the Creole and French (or English if in the diaspora) curriculum can assist the students in their cultural preservation and also the linguistic education for equal opportunities (Kowalski et al., 2022). Religious, educational programs that are started based on the Bible aspire to infuse biblical principles into the learning process and academics for the growth of the overall character of the child as well as the development of godly character (Karim et al., 2022). This may mean including Bible stories in their language arts unit, analyzing a moral dilemma in terms of biblical values in social studies, or examining faith-based science in science.

Because the formal education of some students may be unavoidable, initiatives can also target creating materials and projects for learners with learning disabilities or physical impairments. Such an approach guarantees that each of the community members will be able to get an education from the particular programs. Integrating parents into the education of their children is very important for the years to come (Kowalski et al., 2022). Bible-based interventions include conducting parent education meetings and awareness, the formation of parent-teacher associations, and family contributions to school functions (Guzmán et al., 2020). This, in turn, helps achieve students' success, as well as enhances the community's cohesiveness. As primary education is important, secondary and tertiary education and training, when supported, will create a positive effect in the community. This could be the formulation of scholarship schemes for university education, collaboration with polytechnic institutions in the provision of vocational education, or employment-oriented internships where students are placed with firms.

These Christian-based interventions target multiple facets of education and literacy, focusing on building basic education and literate communities (Karim et al., 2022). They know that education is not only about the accumulation of knowledge, reasoning abilities, creativity, and a person's purposeful worldview. The improvement of literacy leads to the acquisition of worthwhile education; this capacity development involves people within the communities to be in a position to respond to local challenges as well as undertake economic development, thereby improving the welfare of society (Guzmán et al., 2020). Thus, the envisaged system of education and promotion of literacy based on biblical values of wisdom and responsible use of resources can become a key to positive and sustainable change in Haitian local communities and their diaspora.

3. Healthcare and Wellness Programs

Medical and health improvement plans are essentials of all biblical mission outreach services, especially to the Haitian populace, since quality healthcare is not easily accessible to many of them. These programs are designed to work to solve some of the most compelling universal health issues while concurrently providing pastoral care, which paints the picture of a comprehensive approach to man's wholeness, hence, healing as commanded in the scriptures (Deshommes et al., 2020). Of all the strategies that may be used to target specific healthcare needs, the most effective one is the provision of community health clinics. These are small clinics that give out first-level medical care, preventive services, and education to the populace that has the least access to healthcare facilities

(Lansing et al., 2023). In Haiti, where health care is rare and especially in remote areas, the mobilized clinics have greatly increased the population's access to health care services. Such clinics do not only address urgent health conditions but also provide curative and preventive services, as well as health promotion and demotion services, implying a decrease in the prevalence of diseases in the community.

It is also recommended that local people be trained to act as community health workers. These workers can be prepared to impart rudimentary health information, carry out easy health assessments, and play an intermediary role for other diseases when such services are required. This approach is very beneficial because it prevents diseases, enhances health, generates employment for the people of the region, and is also culturally appropriate, besides being sustainable for healthcare missions (Deshommes et al., 2020). Since maternal and infant mortality is high in Haiti, prospects related to maternal and child health will matter a lot. These could comprise an antenatal clinic, nutrition information for pregnant women, child immunization crusades, and postnatal childcare services (Klarman et al., 2021). Fostering such practices may be supplemented by prayer and counseling in addition to treatment since people's physical and spiritual welfare cannot be separated.

Most of the diseases affecting the Haitian population zones are a result of poor water, sanitation, and hygiene amenities. These root causes can be countered by means of Bible-based interventions that include WASH programs focusing on building access to safe water, constructing latrines, and conducting health promotion on hygiene (Lantagne et al., 2021). These efforts can be associated with stewardship lessons and the way a person's body must be treated as the temple of the Holy Spirit. Some of the major barriers Haiti has faced regarding communicable diseases are cholera, HIV/AIDS, and COVID-19. Health-related goals can be achieved by designing programs aimed at education and immunization drives in as many illness-related areas as possible, as well as supporting the affected persons (Klarman et al., 2021). This may encompass physical, spiritual, and emotional well-being for patients and their dependents since it is understood that the element of end-of-life care also involves the patient's welfare.

Mental health is considered to be on the periphery of community health, although it is a fundamental aspect of health.

Thus, programs based on the Bible can provide services such as counseling, which can combine help from ordinary psychologists and specialists in religious beliefs (Karim et al., 2022). This can be especially important in treating traumas than in other communities, given the fact that Haiti has frequently experienced natural disasters, political crises, and economic issues that often result in a significant part of its population being traumatized. Other interventions that have to be included in healthcare interventions are nutrition and food security programs for the Haitian population (Klarman et al., 2021). Examples of such interventive strategies may comprise nutrition education interventions, community gardening, and food distribution. They cover the area of nutrition and hunger, and in doing so, they fit the health and welfare of people and, at the same time, make it possible to teach such gospel values as the provision and love for the neighbor's body and soul.

Preventive care is often more effective and less costly than treating illness after it occurs. The information, awareness, or learning could be focused on simple sanitation and diets for sexually transmitted diseases and long-term sicknesses. These can be provided through community meetings, educational settings, church activities, and several others; this will involve the provision of health information along with religious teachings regarding the proper use and care of God's creations (Miner & Bickerton, 2020). As much as it is a task to encourage the latest health care, it is also actionable to identify the significance of traditional Haitian medical practices beneficial for health and culture. Efforts derived from biblical principles can strive to incorporate such practices where necessary in the enhancement of the individual's physical, mental, social, and spiritual well-being, practicing medicine in harmony with the cultural beliefs of the people (Lowe, 2023). Despite the low literacy rates in Haiti, these healthcare and wellness programs informed by the Scripture are designed to attack adverse facets of the people's physical, mental, and spiritual health with a view of crafting holistic and lasting solutions in those communities. They understand that being healthy is much more than just not being sick; it means being free from infirmity, being strong, emotionally stable, and even religious. By so doing, the target communities are able to manage their own health, hence leading to improved societies of the future.

4. Economic Empowerment and Job Creation

In modern society, socioeconomic growth and employment opportunities are crucial goals in biblical community work, especially for the needy Haitian population suffering from poverty and high unemployment levels. They originate from theoretical angles, religious and Biblical notions of stewardship, productivity, and the tendency of the weak and vulnerable to establish viability in the economy (Lowe, 2023). A good strategy for economic enfranchisement is the microfinance initiatives that offer funds to persons who cannot secure credit from conventional financial institutions. These programs can be designed in ways that provide biblical provisions when it comes to lending and stewardship, and finance provides not only cash but also guidance and knowledge (Miner & Bickerton, 2020). Since these programs assist individuals in starting or expanding units of small businesses, they will create employment opportunities for people and boost the economy of a region.

Offering vocational training and skills development enables the person to acquire relevant inputs to seek employment or engage in their own income-generating activities. It is important to note that

Bible-based initiatives can provide courses in areas such as carpentry, stitching, farming, car repair, and information services (Lowe, 2023). Such programs generally include principles from the scriptures, such as the importance of hard work, quality work, and work as worship. Since agriculture is a primary industry in Haiti and the livelihood of many citizens, any programs that seek to strengthen farmers or enhance farming could be effective (Elusma et al., 2022). This might entail offering an education on the use of new and efficient methods of farming, giving seeds, implements, or inputs to the farmers, or assisting in forming organizations that enable farmers to get a better price for their produce. These can be associated with biblical concepts of tilling the land and the proper and noble way of earning from the soil.

Ethical trade includes fair wages and decent working conditions for workers; hence, supporting this practice is an important cause. Bible-based ventures can assist in the creation of organizations supporting businesses consistent with these principles, especially those relating to coffee, cocoa, or arts and crafts vital to the Haitian economy (Elusma et al., 2022). Financial education can be defined as the skills and enlightenment of people in making sound monetary decisions in different aspects of life since many in the Haitian communities may not fully understand how to handle what they earn. The identified Bible-based programs can provide individuals with financial education courses where, for example, information about budgeting, saving, and reasonable borrowing can be given with reference to the principles of the Bible (Guzmán et al., 2020). Job training and placement services are considered the vital building blocks of economic empowerment. Programs created on the basis of biblical truths may help develop programs that are designed to prepare people for certain sectors or positions and then help find employers for them (Kanat-Maymon et al., 2020). This might involve obtaining sponsorship, advertisement, and cooperation with some of the existing companies in the community, facilitating job fairs, or directing the participants to companies that offer such services in order to help them write their resumes and prepare for interviews.

The emergence of the filled and incubator-like stations of development supports the ideas of potential owners who can create new workplaces for people in Haitian communities. These incubators offer physical space and can also offer support to the entrepreneurs in terms of training and provision of resources to support the businesses inside them (Kanat-Maymon et al., 2020). They can promote a biblical perspective on doing business and serving society. Through the application of these numerous strategies in economic empowerment and job creation, Bible-based projects contribute positively to financial sustainability and the worth of Haitian people (Lowe, 2023). All of these efforts remember that it is not prosperity alone that entails the development of wealth, but it also seeks to allow the people to develop the talents that have been endowed to them by the Lord, to be supportive roles to the community, and to be able to provide for their families.

5. *Community Infrastructure and Development*

Community infrastructure and development are essential in enhancing the well-being of individuals within their places of residence and even in other parts of the world. These factors are even more pronounced in a country such as Haiti, which has encountered many problems over the years. The Haitian people, including those living domestically, and the international community, including Haitian expatriates around the globe, feel the impacts of infrastructure and development in multiple spheres, both momentary or repeated on a regular basis and over the long term (Kowalski et al., 2022). Thus, in Haiti, the state of all community infrastructural facilities can meet only an insignificant percentage of the population's demand. In many places, the roads are bad, if existent at all; the water systems are poor or nonexistent; the electricity grids are inadequate, and many buildings in the public domain are dilapidated. The absence of these basic structures slows economic development, complicates the education and healthcare systems, and hinders the improvement of people's living standards. First, the Bible supports the concept of prudent planning and construction, as seen in Proverbs 24:3, whereby Solomon notes that through wisdom, understanding, and knowledge, houses (indicated to mean communities) are established (King James Version, 2019).

Well-established social structures show progress in terms of quality of living standards, health aspects of the community, and economic development. When people of the community have a good quality water supply from sources such as boreholes, adequate electricity supply, and a good network of roads, then such communities are able to conduct businesses, provide education, and improve their health status. This can be attributed to biblical stewardship, where humans are commanded to be accountable for the resources, including the environment that was provided by God (Karim et al., 2022). The thoughts about infrastructure and development in the host country and its relation to Haitian peoples living in foreign nations are perceived as more antithetical to those in their native country. In the host countries, Haitian immigrants get exposed to well-developed infrastructure and thus receive suitable living conditions, but at the same time, they obtain awareness about the drawbacks of Haiti faced by their fellow citizens (Klarman et al., 2021). It is mainly drawn from the experience gained through long-time Hardship in the host. Country, this makes the diaspora contribute to the development efforts in Haiti; this shall promote the virtue of neighborly love, which is proximate to Christian teaching.

The improvement of the community infrastructure is also a reflection of social and spiritual qualities. Temples, community halls, and schools are some of the essential structures that help Haitians both inside and outside of Haiti. These institutions not only offer opportunities for meeting in real life but also create social relations and support people in preserving traditions and spiritual values. The church is also very central to Christians through fellowship, as stated in Hebrews 10:24-25, which encourages believers to assemble together and compel one another to do acts of love and good deeds (King James Version, 2019). Haiti works to build the communities' basic physical and social structures, which are much needed for problems such as natural disasters, political instability, and lack of capital, among others. Nevertheless, there are progressive processes in Haiti that have resulted from the activity of the local population, international organizations, and Haitians living abroad (Kowalski et al., 2022). Such initiatives generally are targeted at sustainable development, which means the practice of development that helps to enhance the welfare of the target population.

Thus, the concept of community infrastructure and development covers not only tangible structures that create a framework for enabling social processes and improving people's quality of life but also the processes that occur within this framework. As for the Haitian case, the advancements in these aspects may result in decreased rates of poverty, improved levels of health, and an enhanced ability to cope with difficulties. Haitian communities in the Diaspora have adequate support and development in host countries; hence, the foundation on which this set of people establishes meaningful lives and integration in their new countries, they still have a bond with Haiti (Naidu et al., 2021). The church, faith, and organizational unity also help the Haitian communities to move forward and enhance infrastructure and development within Haiti as well as other countries. It is in this context that biblically derived aspects of wisdom in construction practices, efficient use of resources, love for one's neighbor, and the role of community support underpin these endeavors (Lowe, 2023). Through practicing sustainable and community-oriented development, Haitians are striving for change and, at the same time, improving the existing living conditions and the quality of life of future generations, reflecting the core cultural and spiritual values of Haiti.

6. Social Justice and Advocacy

Social justice and advocacy are critical in the development of societies and fighting for equality within a society and at the international level. To the Haitian community, these concepts are relevant because of the country's historical background, including colonialism, political crises, and economic problems (Charles, 2020). Therefore, social justice and advocacy are both fundamental principles of the Biblical teachings and were washed with the principles of justice for all and protection of the oppressed. Since the context involves Haiti, the social justice consideration would all be subsumed under the banner of social justice, and it comprises issues like poverty, education, health, and equity, amongst others. These issues have particularly magnified the country's social impacts, affecting the people in their daily lives and in the future. Proverbs, Isaiah, and similar books of the Bible are specific with the concern to teach justice and care for the needy (King James Version, 2019). These truths, therefore, offer a guide as to how different injustices that are experienced by many people in Haiti are to be dealt with.

Organizational advocacy within Haiti is mainly directed towards raising living standards, protecting the rights of individuals, and aiming at the enhancement of economies. Non-governmental organizations, churches, other non-profit organizations, and civil society associations remain relevant in advocating for people's causes and issues. These attempts refer to the Scriptural passage Speak up for the dumb and do justice to him that suffers oppression from Proverbs (King James Version, 2019). For instance, by advocating for the voiceless and struggling for the rights of the oppressed, advocates in Haiti fight for justice and, at the same time, fulfill the principles of their faith. Haitian citizens who relocate to other countries are very influential in the fight for human rights and social justice both in their new nations and in Haiti as well. Today, many Haitians live in foreign countries, and the majority of them hold quite powerful positions or have significant amounts of money that they use in fighting for better policies towards Haiti, more funds to be sent there, and to work for better treatment of Haitian immigrants (Charles, 2020). This global social advocacy is based on the biblical injunction of the golden rule, which posits the love of one's neighbor. The idea of community is broadened to include other people anywhere in the world.

Haitians who moved to other countries in search of refuge seek social justice and political activism mostly revolves around the same aspects as in other immigrant communities, such as integration, rights, and non-discrimination (Trott et al., 2020). Language problems, as well as cultural and sometimes ethnic hostility, are always evident in Haitian immigrants. In such settings, advocacy endeavors seek to promote equal opportunities, access to services, and appreciation for the positive roles that Haitians bring to their new places of dwelling. These efforts correspond to such a biblical concept as hospitality towards the stranger as well as toward every person. Social justice, together with advocacy, has a quantitative influence on the lives of Haitian groups (Salusky et al., 2020). Achievable goals result in enhanced standards of living, educational facilities, and earning capabilities. In Haiti, this could come in the form of developed infrastructure, better health care, and better resource distribution. Haitian communities have to gain the upper hand when they manage to get the attention of their respective host countries' governments, thus leading to better policies as well as integration programs and cultural sensitivity.

However, it should be noted that the fight for social justice and the promotion of advocacy work are not without their difficulties. Haitian interventions are sometimes less efficient due to political crises, lack of funding, and the size of the problems faced (Salusky et al., 2020). While engaging in advocacy, advocates may come across either apathy from authorities and the populace back home or opposition. Nevertheless, the Haitian community does not back down through the hardships of society but relies on faith and the Haitian Spirit (Trott et al., 2020). Deology and theology found in Christianity are often regarded as motivations to support social justice and advocacy in the Haitian populace. Religious tenets containing creeds of God's favor to the poor, the need to practice justice, and the law of love as a guide to the treatment of neighbors and self. These teachings motivate the people as well as the communities to strive to gain a just society despite the existing hardships.

7. Environmental Stewardship and Sustainability

Global environmental consciousness and sustainable development are worthy causes that affect communities across the globe, including the Haitian community (Kump, 2023). In Haiti, a country that owns marvelous views of nature but is facing several environmental issues, these concepts are important. Another primary cause of concern is spirituality, and the Bible is the most dominant source of spirituality that gives any human being guidance on how to take care of the earth; God gave Adam the mantle to exercise dominion on the face of the earth (King James Version, 2019). On a practical level, this prophetic view of the Bible is applied to contemporary environmental issues, advocating for the management and proper usage of resources. In Haiti, environmental issues are strongly connected with social and economic problems. Issues such as deforestation, soil erosion, water pollution, and natural disasters actually influence the everyday Haitians' lives. From the above environmental problems, it is evident that they worsen poverty, affect agricultural yield, and cause health complications (Yuriev et al., 2020). Therefore, this book proposes applying the theological theory of stewardship to navigate through these challenges because it integrates the human being with the environment.

Some of the ways through which the people of Haiti have attempted to achieve environmental sustenance include afforestation, ecological agriculture, and proper disposal of waste. Such programs go further in that they seek to restore the ecosystem as well as promote the development of sustainable practices among the population (Yuriev et al., 2020). Such approaches are, therefore, in harmony with the principles of handling resources as contained in the Bible and the plight of the needy. They help meet society's demands for sustainable practices by performing their stewardship to the creation of Haitians. Environmentalism is a worldwide issue, and this means that environmental problems do not confine themselves to a particular country or boundary; Haitian communities living in other countries are also affected (Kump, 2023). Haitians in the diaspora still have a love for their home country, and as such, they care about the effects of the environment. This concern turns to funding environmental activities in the Haitian environment, sharing information, and lobbying. The provisions and extensions of care across nation borders portray the scripture that says one should love their neighbor even from afar.

In new countries where Haitians have constructed their social existence, the culture of managing the environment is an implication of social existence. Considering the current environmental practices and laws in the countries that Haitian immigrants get to live in, it will be different. Therefore, the challenge for these societies and cultures when transposing such principles into new contexts and paradigms is complicated by the need to do so while not totally abandoning the same values and their focus on the stewardship of environments (Mombeuil, 2020). Haitians participate in many community-related environmental issues in their adopted countries, with the lenses inherited from their home country. The responsibilities that are outlined for the people in the environment also include intergenerational ones, which are supported by the Bible. Psalms even use the phrase to convey the calling to tell future generations of the Lord's works, which would encompass the preservation of the natural world (King James Version, 2019). For Haitian communities, this means having a responsibility to look after the environment not only for the present generation but also for the future. It is such a long-term view that is needed for the sustainable development processes in Haiti as well as in the Haitian diaspora.

The challenges of environmental sustainability, such as inadequate and competing resources, climate change, and its other repercussions, are evident in Haiti. However, there are also good projects implemented by the local population, international organizations, and Haitian immigrants. These may involve a fusion of cultural people's beliefs with scientific and technological practices in a holistic and physiological concept of conservation or stewardship based on the Bible (King James Version, 2019). Environmental stewardship and sustainability have various effects on Haitian communities (Mombeuil, 2020). A better environment significantly reduces the rate of diseases, increases agricultural yields, and increases the ability to cope with natural disasters. In Haiti, this can play a role in poverty alleviation and the growth of the economy. Regarding the Haitian communities in the diaspora, which have environmental issues as a topic of interest, participation could lead to identification with the Haitian culture and, therefore, a possibility of being an active part of the society in host countries.

8. Cultural Preservation and Arts

Culture and fine art are critical components of society and significant, influential factors that contribute to hierarchy as well as success when it comes to coping with adverse situations in a universal society. These aspects assume greater value given the background of the Haitian community in terms of the cultural and artistic color that the people take pride in. Religion as a culture does not have principles touching on cultural preservation but has principles that support heritage, creativity, and community expression as trends in the Bible. These concepts of the Bible form the basis of the importance of culture and arts in Haitian society as well as among the Haitians in the diaspora. In this context, the preservation of culture in Haiti is a process closely connected to the struggle and liberation (Minn, 2020). Like many other Caribbean islands, Haiti has a rich cultural agenda that can also be described as complex and diverse, which has been developing due to the interaction of African, Tano, and French people. The cultural identity in question finds excellent expression through the arts: music, dancing, painting, and literature (Boutros, 2020). Most biblical teachings, especially those of the Old Testament, stress the need to remember and relay the culture and traditions of one's people (King James Version, 2019). Thus, for Haitians, the role of the arts is not solely to maintain traditions but also to celebrate Haiti's social existence against all odds.

Haitian painting is an important and unique tradition of Haitian visual art; this type of art is characterized by bright colors, spiritual themes, and dealing with social issues. Some Haitian artists paint and sculpt on meanings related to Vodou, historical aspects, and even current lives, therefore depicting the diversified Haitian culture (Minn, 2020). In this context, one might consider this form of art as a form of food stewardship insofar as artists employ the talents that they received from the divine to document and appreciate cultural assets (Boutros, 2020). The scripture also instructs its believers to keep using one's talents for the benefit of society, and Haitian artists do that to the letter.

Music and dance are very important facets of Haitian society, customs, and festivities, as they are performed during rituals, parties, and official functions. Subgenres such as Kompa, Rara, and Mizik Rasin would encompass African beats with European melodies, hence unique Haitian music (Boutros, 2020). Such musical forms occasionally contain religious themes, which speak of the pure belief of the Haitian people. The Psalms of the Old Testament also include an account of music and dancing in praise and in the conduct of the congregation, which proclaims revelations for the function of arts that are music and dance in culture and tradition (King James Version, 2019). In Haitian populations, for instance, within the Diaspora, culture, and art become vital since they play a role in how the immigrants stay connected to their origin and in how the new generations learn and embrace Haitian native culture (Minn, 2020). Haitian people can also start businesses and contribute to the community, building structures and supporting arts and culture to fulfill cultural needs, which in turn keeps their culture alive despite living in other countries. These efforts of preserving and integrating Haiti's culture with other cultures also correspond with biblical teachings on hospitality, as most of these programs are initiated to welcome newcomers into the culture and to sensitize other people about Haiti's culture.

The role in portraying Haitian cultural preservation and arts cannot be underestimated. In Haiti, such actions increase nationalism, create the ability for cultural tourism, or contribute to the social fabric. The arts give something for a society to work through, something for them to triumph over, and something for them that will depict a better tomorrow. In foreign states where Haitian populations live, cultural sustenance serves to keep up the Haitian cultural heritage yet also enhances the cultural diversity of the countries (Boutros, 2020). But cultural preservation in Haiti remains an issue trying to fight things like poverty, political misdirection, and the glitz of modern popular culture among the youth. Despite these barriers, there are Haitians who strive to carry forward the culture of the country and bequeath it to the ensuing generations in the most suitable manner possible (Minn, 2020). This is the students' desire to remain faithful to what they are in the midst of tough circumstances, the same way the Israelites had to during their exile. Some of the most promising areas of influence for Haitians include cultural sustenance and art since they have social effects within Haiti and among the Haitian populace in other countries. Distilled from biblical notions of legacy, artistry, and people's voices, these endeavors exist to sustain affirmation, rebuild strength, and build a cultural rapport (Boutros, 2020). Such problems may exist, but the dedication to maintaining their culture and arts shows the Haitians' and other related communities' spirit of strength, faith, and creativity.

9. Youth Empowerment and Mentorship

Youth empowerment and the provision of mentorship play a very important role in the development of the societies that they belong to in their current and future contexts. When applied to the Haitian community, these conceptions are especially meaningful because Haiti is rather a young country, and the young population faces so many problems (Neufeldt & Janzen, 2020). There is, therefore, evident and direct scriptural support for the issues of youth guidance and support and, by extension, the support of youth empowerment and youth mentoring in today's Haitian society and in the societies of the Haitian Diaspora. In Haiti, more than 50% of its population is under the age of twenty-five, making youth employment and mentoring critical to tackling socioeconomic vices (Neufeldt & Janzen, 2020). Haitians today have an uncertain future for reasons such as poor education standards, low employment rates, and insecurity. The teachings of Proverbs regarding wisdom and Jesus's conduct with his disciples, pointing out the need to fester the young, indicate that benign stake in youth (King James Version, 2019). Key findings have indicated that through promoting youths and training them, Haitian communities are aiming at constructing a better future.

The main activities that are associated with youth empowerment in Haiti include education, training on various skills, and leadership. These programs are focused on empowering youths so that they can face difficulties and become productive citizens in society. Hence, such efforts are biblical, especially when it comes to the understanding of stewardship and the management of talents. Through the development of youth's capacities and encouraging them to achieve their goals, these endeavors represent an example of the biblical call to walk in one's destiny. Another key to youth development is mentorship, where youth can find direction from and positive models to emulate (Neufeldt & Janzen, 2020). Given the fact that most families in Haiti might have been affected by one factor or another, such as the economy, disasters, or migration, personal examples may hold the young people tightly, especially through mentorship schemes. This sort of mentorship is similar to the biblical relationships like that of Apostle Paul and Timothy, where Paul, the senior and experienced person, offers his guidance and support to the junior and less experienced Timothy in the practical areas of life and spirituality (King James Version, 2019).

Thus, youth inclusion and mentorship further play other roles within Haitian societies in other countries. Current young generation Haitians in other countries they live continue to be faced with cultural conflicts regarding their Haitian roots and the culture of the countries in which they now live. Mentorship programs in these contexts, therefore, aim at preserving culture, academic achievement, and career advancement. They are illustrating the scripture put down in the Holy Bible along the lines of one generation, one memory being handed down to the next generation, with the aim of helping the young Haitians to stay rooted while bearing the burden of the new world (King James Version, 2019). The benefits of youth empowerment and absorption by Haitian-based mentors affect so many communities. Youth with empowered status, therefore, are fully aware of their rights and are determined to exercise their political liberties in accessing education as well as participating in determining matters of society (Neufeldt & Janzen, 2020). In Haiti, this can mean more employment for youths, better communication and relationships between different groups in Haitian society, and genuine leaders being born at the right time to help Haiti overcome its problems. Youth empowerment programs are vital, especially for the Haitian communities in foreign nations, because they give young people the chance to be empowered and receive the assistance and means they require within the adopted countries while at the same time continuing to embrace the Haitian culture.

Nonetheless, there are various challenges affecting youth empowerment and mentoring in Haiti, such as inadequate funding, poverty, and political instability. Nevertheless, there are still numerous people and organizations that encourage the development of young people, citing biblical messages that encourage endurance and expectation (Neufeldt & Janzen, 2020). The performance depicted by the Haitian youths and their mentors when faced with adversity portrays faith related to the scriptures. This paper explores several Haitian youth empowerment programs, as the New Testament model of youth being under the care of the community is also practiced in Haiti (King James Version, 2019). Leaders and demographically, the youth require guidance and support, which is mostly provided by churches, community-based organizations, and people from the diaspora. This concept of youth development as a collective responsibility responds to the Holy Scriptures' model of the church as a family where people encourage one another.

As Haitian communities go all out to empower young ones and mentor them, they are also funding a future that belongs to those young ones and the entire nation. They try the combined notions of the Bible about children and youths, who are considered a blessing and a burden. This has given a clear insight as to how the Haitian communities are doing their best to ensure that young people are empowered so that they do not continue living in poverty but rather get an opportunity to learn how to transform their lives as well as their community by building needed skills and asset knowledge. Thus, youth engagement and mentorship have great effects on Haitian citizens as well as on other foreign nations (Neufeldt & Janzen, 2020). Born out of the scriptures for direction, accountability, and community welfare, these movements aim at fostering and developing the youth for leadership roles in society. Indeed, there are still problems, but constant efforts aimed at youths' and young people's engagement in the leadership and mentoring processes are examples of hope, faith, and optimism inherent in Haitian people and their international counterparts (Lowe, 2023). Therefore, these activities demonstrate that rather than mere responses to current common challenges, Haitians embarked on measures that would help create a better future.

10. Community Reconciliation and Peace building

Community reconciliation and peace building are important processes in healing societal pain and building reconciliation in communities, both in Haiti and in Haitian communities around the world. These concepts are based on religious aspects, especially the biblical principles of forgiveness, reconciliation, and the fight for peace (Lowe, 2023). Haiti is a conflicted society in the context of constantly changing polities and power struggles; therefore, reconciliation and other related activities are important for the country to implement. Members of the Haitian community had to overcome many obstacles that caused social tensions to arise and fracture Haitian society (Beckett, 2020). Achieving unity within a society is a process that has to be cultivated due to political instabilities within the country, economic inequalities, and social prejudices resulting from past injustices.

The Bible has instructions with regard to such matters as it propounded the principles of striving for peace and of following the paths of reconciliation as demonstrated by Jesus and the apostles. Indeed, it seems that the reconciliation that occurs in Haitian communities generally consists of overcoming the divisions stemming from social, economic, and political differences. Such measures might include the sharing of stories, dialogues, social and community activities, as well as other activities that encourage the reconciliation of former rivals (Anthony, 2023). These approaches tally with the teachings of Scripture, for the main cause of the quarrel and contention is to apply a peacemaker who resolves the matter personally (Lowe, 2023). The other dimension of peace in the Haitian context entails dealing with underlying causes of conflict, which include poverty, illiteracy, and resource imbalance. In striving for such societies, Haitian communities are living up to the word of God and following the injunctions of righteousness and justice coupled with the protection of the needy. All these endeavors reflect the scripture's social justice themes and the establishment of good societies.

For Haitians living in other countries, particularly in the United States, the Caribbean, Canada, and Europe, the concept of reconciliation and peace building is broader. Such may encompass reconciliation of the diaspora with one another, reconciliation of the different generations of immigrants, as well as improved relations with other groups in Asian countries or any other country they belong to (Ciorciari, 2022). These efforts correspond to the Bible phrase about being in harmony with all, which is pointed out in the New Testament (King James Version, 2019). Reconciliation and peacebuilding efforts in the Haitian setting affect the communities significantly. Positive goals may result in increased unity and coordination in the fight against common problems and a decrease in violent tendencies. This could be the case in Haiti, where leadership will be more stable, and plans for community development will be implemented well. For Haitian communities living and working abroad, it can create stronger, more coherent diaspora organizations and be more capable of helping other members and contributing towards positive, effect-worthy societies.

Nevertheless, reconciliation and peace building are never easy or quick tasks but rather a continuing and gradual process towards the restoration of people's relations. It entails dedication to the processes and acceptance to confront some pertinent challenges. Two biblical notions, the endurance of suffering and salvation through love, are optimism and the directions for anyone dealing with this kind of work. Haitian people are slowly moving towards the process of rebuilding their nation and forgiving one another; they have faith and hope in their culture (Anthony, 2023). Haitians are following the scriptural urge to be phronemataeschatai, that is, peacemakers and reconcilers; in doing this, they are not merely healing a nation's trauma but are also developing the structure of a healthy society (Ciorciari, 2022). Such actions reflect the hope, faith, and voiced determination that Haitians in Haiti and Haitian constituencies abroad embody.

Conclusion

Altogether, these ten biblical strategies for transforming communities with reference to the Haitian context provide a widespread approach to effective biblical change. These initiatives aim to transform society by providing solutions to spiritual, educational, economic, environmental, and social issues in a way that would enable society and its individuals to overcome all challenges and attain a better future (Karim et al., 2022). These approaches are rooted in the principles of love, justice, and stewardship that are found in the Bible and are focused on the physical, but also the spiritual, enhancement of the lives of people and the need to bring justice to society (King James Version, 2019). In the course of these enactments, people should not forget to look at themselves with humility and respect for cultural diversity and as collaborators working with the local communities, as change is a process that happens through God at His due time by people who are willing to take the stand.

CHAPTER 5

You Are Born to Lead!

In the Haitian culture, especially within the Haitian community, people strongly believe that everyone is born with leadership genes. This conviction is not merely an academic belief but a ground reality that defines the capacity of Haitians to position and locate themselves and, consequently, their functions in families, neighborhoods, and the nation. It is important to note that Haitian children, especially from an early age, are encouraged and nurtured to celebrate the gifts that are within them, for they know that they have been endowed with the ability to transform their world (Barrow, 2022). The belief stems from the Haitian community that, as believers of the Holy Scripture, each person is created in the likeness of God and, therefore, has a leadership capacity in them (Lowe, 2023). A bright example of this type of Haitian-American is Wyclef Jean. Wyclef Jean, the musician, producer, and activist, has been on the frontlines fighting for the improvement of Haiti. He has also used his stardom and wallet to reach out to his community and start programs offering relief and assistance in areas of education, health, and disaster. Wyclef inspired a lot of Haitians, in Haiti and outside, and made the latter realize that they, too, can be leaders of their society and become active for the common good.

According to Haitian culture, which is dynamically developing now, every person is born as a leader, and this idea is fostered consciously. It is not merely a principle that is idealistic but rather an actuality translated into a daily belief through which the Haitian people now look at themselves and their respective assignments in their homes, communities, and the entire nation (Alexander, 2021). Diaspora Haitian children grow up with the principle or belief that they have gifts and potentials, talents that make them distinct from other people and which enable them to change their world (Lansing et al., 2023). This belief is based on the Haitian people's strong narrative of creation, where the essence of existence is based on the biblical creation, where each person has the image of God and the potential for creativity, wisdom, and purpose.

In order to follow up on the Haitian people's understanding of themselves as God's children, this segment reminds the Haitian people of the importance of realizing their potential and doing what

God has destined them to do in life (Karim et al., 2022). The community entails its members searching for their potential, listening to the call, discovering the special graces that have been given to a person, and utilizing these gifts to serve themselves and the family, neighborhood, and nation at large. The focus on one's leadership qualities is not for the cultivation of selfishness and egocentric nature, but it is an attempt to change the Haitian people's perceptions and make them understand that they are important and they contain potential that can be useful to their society (Kanat-Maymon et al., 2020). The community comes to realize that when every individual responds to their calling, then the amplified effects mirror the potential of the people's talents in positively transforming a nation when the appropriate solutions to the challenges affecting it are developed.

The Haitian community looks to biblical figures as the leaders who accepted their call for the divine purpose with a view to achieving great transformations. They draw examples from Joseph, chosen by God to go and free his brethren from the land of Egypt, or Esther, who literally put her life on the line to save her people from extermination. These are some of the stories that will help everyone understand that leadership is not one's vocation for the chosen few but a call that responds to everyone. While the Haitian community rejoices in dancing and observing the apparent prominence of the members in leadership roles, they also embrace them, calling for their calling and support to effectively develop them. It unites managers, professional educators, and practical key resources within a community to foster skills and knowledge in every person in order to be successful at leading change within their organizational niches (Lowe, 2023). Whether it is a young man or woman aspiring to own a successful business, a community leader who is struggling to improve the lives of the needy people back in Haiti or a teacher who dreams of seeing their students change the world, Haitian people are, as a whole, people who believe in changing society and being changers (Minn, 2020). Group emphasis on leadership significantly impacts one's self as well as the tapestry of Haitian society. When more Haitians come to a point in their lives where they surrender to their destiny and claim the spots in leadership, the ripples of change start being felt in the society, and each speck of that change is contributed to by every leader. In the Haitian community, the concept of "you are born to lead" is not rhetoric but a verity that dictates clients' day-to-day existence. This is a belief that makes people develop their gifts from God, look for ways of volunteering to serve, and strive hard to change society for the better (Miner & Bickerton, 2020). In this positive synergy, the people of Haiti are expected to deliver positive and significant results towards the nation's progress as emancipating light bearers of changes in the years to come.

Do Not Be Afraid to Take Risks

Categorized under ethno entrepreneurship, the Haitian community appreciates a courage-based risk-taking mentality, even when it comes to establishing new businesses, the sole idea of which represents a type of risk for new beginnings as well as for the emergence of the unknown (Johnson, 2021). This mode of thinking may be attributed to the Haitian people's strong faith and the concept of divine providence, which dictates that the creator of a person has a plan for that person's life. Haitians are to embrace life as they approach everything with vigor and courage, knowing that fear is not an option in people's pursuit of their destiny. This spirit of risk-taking is well captured by Haitian Americans, one of whom is the renowned artist Jean-Michel Basquiat. Even with his unarguable talent as an artist, Basquiat was a pioneer who did not' fit' into the art world of the time and went on to create his very own style, fusing graffiti, neo-expressionism, and social commentary (Garay et al., 2022). Despite the critics and society not accepting him in the first place and even denying him the basic necessities and support most artists had at that time, Basquiat endured and left a huge impact as one of the greatest artists of his time (Garay et al., 2022). He courageously challenges authorities to innovate and personally encourages thousands of Haitians to develop their creative talents and to work hard to realize one's dreams.

When exploring the Haitian people's way of life within the context of American society, one can observe that courage and risk-taking are at the forefront of the Haitian community. The Haitian population is not ignorant of the fact that in personal and even societal development, one has to be ready to go out of their comfort zone. This thinking is instilled in them from heart, faith, and probably the belief that God has a plan for their lives (Miner & Bickerton, 2020). In this context, the Haitian community reinforces the principle of embracing life through the enthusiasm and conceptualization of risk-taking and seeking the unknown in achieving one's goals and destiny. This ethos was taken from the biblical saying in the book of Proverbs that the righteous shall be like a lion, thereby constantly reminding the Haitian citizens that one should never move without confidence and determination (King James Version, 2019).

Therefore, when it comes to Haitian culture, the act of risk-taking is not defined as 'throwing caution to the wind' but rather refers to the act of courageously charting a course towards worthwhile goals. They understand that if they want to become great, they have to leave their comfort zone and get down to the things they have no control over. This might mean beginning a new career, going back to school, or even assuming a formal leadership position in one's community—all enterprises that require the courage to accept the risk that is implicit in change (Lansing et al., 2023). For the Haitian people, therefore, the higher level of risk-taking to which they are being led in this process of reinvention requires a process of discernment. They come to elders, community authorities, and their faith both in themselves and in God (Lowe, 2023). They assess the opportunities and threats with proficiency, and they proceed to make the right decisions that respect their perspectives, the well-being of their community, and the purpose that God has predestined them for.

In Haitian Americans' case, the degree of calculated risk that is reflected in their business demeanor is palpable. This new venture is not a hindrance to the people to whom they keep on developing their ideas, sense of creativity, and hard-working spirit that is needed in initiating a new company. They comprehend that the road to successful businessmen is not always linear, but they do believe that their readiness to take risks combined with the further development of the economy leads to the achievement of a higher level of prosperity and more privatization (Neufeldt & Janzen, 2020). In the same manner as the future in the aspect of education, the Haitian community challenges its members to take a shot at post-secondary education, irrespective of pursuing education away from home (Kump, 2023). They understand that knowledge and skill are precious capital that they are willing to bet on since they prepare them to competently fix the problems that affect societies.

Thus, as the Haitian people have adopted this kind of mindset, they are able to see the results of courage in the Haitian's individual life and the life of the community. Formerly, people hardly decided to come forward and offer their skills and abilities to meet the requirements in their neighborhoods. Companies that used to act conservatively today invest and diversify, thus contributing to employment and gross domestic product (Lansing et al., 2023). Therefore, the entire nation, which has for long been crushed under the uncertainty of the future, finds itself rising in unison in the search for a better tomorrow. The imaginative spirit of risk affirmation is not only restricted to business challenges; it applies to the Haitian population's social and community life as well (Kowalski et al., 2022). It describes the population as daring, as open to eschew traditional ways, do not hesitate to fight for change, and embrace voicing their opinion against the prevailing vices. They know that change is not easy, and sometimes, people have to epitomize courage in order to make necessary changes for the better. They are ready to take the chance and fight for justice.

A rather vivid example of this can be observed in the Haitian people's coping with natural disasters and various other emergencies. God's children, the Haitian people, do not run away in fear or surrender themselves to the calamities of earthquakes and hurricanes (Karim et al., 2022). However, they fly into action, be it physically, financially, or in spirit, using all the available might and desire to alleviate the situation, restore the places that have fallen victim to disaster, and come out even stronger (Naidu et al., 2021). To risk and persevere is definitively part of the Haitian culture and motto shared through generations by the Haitian people. The people comprehend that, with the help of the culture of courageous actions, there is no problem that cannot be solved, and the future will be hopeful, prosperous, and effective.

Spirituality is an essential component of the Haitian approach to embracing risk because these people are Christians who believe in the Creator. They are convinced that the same God who commissions them for leadership and for change in their world will also be their companion and will guide them through the unpredictable terrains of risk-taking by providing them with ideas, strength, and all the resources they need (Miner & Bickerton, 2020). The Haitian people have exhibited such characteristics and are still moving along the path of taking such risks that will transform their lives and probably influence the lives of many others. They continued with their success stories and strength and emphasized the message of courage to their fellow citizens, urging them to come out and produce more of what they hide within them. In the passionate Haitian society, people's readiness for risks is not just an idea but a real-life experience (Neufeldt & Janzen, 2020). It is a belief that enables the people to face their fears and grab the opportunities as well as the chance to shape the future, bearing in mind the great potential of the nation. Thus, by becoming an embodiment of courageous activity, the Haitian population is ready to become pioneers in the making of their communities and become the beacon of change for others.

Do not worry about your haters! Focus on your calling to improve your community.

The Haitian populations know that change and assuming positions of authority require power struggles in the community. When these individuals take their destined roles to work in society, they may incite annoyance or hostility from society or other people due to a lack of acceptance or comprehension of the role of the organisms in society. But the Haitians are living by the philosophy of turning the other cheek, concentrating on the usefulness of their work to society and not on the persecutors' opinions (Trott et al., 2020). One extraordinary example of a Haitian-American who has lived her life with such belief is Edwidge Danticat. Holding the position of a credible author and a successful storyteller, Danticat raised her voice and shared the destinies of the Haitians living in the country as well as Haitians living in other countries (Yi, 2021). Ever since she got into writing, Danticat has also encountered different critiques and doubts from those who do not see or hear the difficulties and triumphs of the Haitian people, especially women, and children, and yet she continues to write to create hope and inspire them. Thus, she has helped thousands of Haitians to stand tall and find purpose in bringing change to their society and being proud of their identity.

In the lively Haitian culture, the culture bearers know too well that leadership and community change are not without some hitches. These characters get up and begin to chase God's purposes for them; they may be confronted with resistance, negative comments, or even hostility from others who do not agree with what they are doing (Karim et al., 2022). However, the Haitian people are endowed with a common sense that is practical and urges them not to be outdone by the ill but to outdo evil with goodness. They understand that paying attention to the negativity and 'haters' will only distract them from the real job ahead—the job of changing the lives of their communities for the better. The Haitian community comprehends that they do not need the approval of anybody but to seize the divine call established in their lives. These cases are motivated by examples from the Scriptures where individuals such as Nehemiah find themselves flooded with criticism when they embark on the assignment of rebuilding the walls of Jerusalem but do not swerve in their determination (King James Version, 2019).

It may be for this reason that Haitian people invest little or no time or energy, dreading what critics may be saying about them, but instead, they work towards the transformation of their society. The central theme is to understand the specific needs and obstacles of their neighborhoods, and then they do their best to come up with original means of solving these problems (Kanat-Maymon et al., 2020). An example of this displeasure can be observed in the community's handling of the persisting issue of urban poverty and inadequate educational opportunities (Klarman et al., 2021). Overcoming all these challenges is difficult; rather than be discouraged, the Haitian people have stood up to the challenge. They have also established educational programs in the community, including after-school, vocational, training centers, and scholarships for needy children so that poor children can spend their school days with quality education (Johnson, 2021). These are not simply the projects of giving handouts or short-term fixes but the projects of cultivating the leaders of tomorrow in Haiti so that they do not fall under the cycle of being impoverished. Likewise, the Haitian community has also provided its support to address the problem of poor health facilities. Instead of merely whining about the scarcity of medical facilities, they have developed community health centers, which are community health clinics and walking hospital programs and have intellectually imparted skills of primary healthcare among the less privileged.

The Haitian people are helping to develop healthier, safer lifestyles while at the same time introducing ideological concepts such as self-reliance and comradeship. They are showing others that leadership is not a position where one gets to be pampered and presented with awards, but it is about utilizing one's skills and any influence one has to positively transform the lives of others (Kanat-Maymon et al., 2020). The Haitians see their community as one that is anointed to be a blessing to others as they keep on witnessing the change that comes about from their encouragement. It can seem that a person cannot make a change, but people who once did not believe in themselves go up as leaders, focusing on their strengths and gifts and exhausting their abilities to solve the problems of their neighborhoods. Once, the startups faced a great deal of difficulties in achieving growth; now, they contribute to economic development and provide people with jobs. And the nation, in general, which was once burdened by the vices of misfortune, is now strong and focused on creating a better tomorrow (Johnson, 2021). The unrelenting commitment to community development is not for select programs or ventures; it is a lifestyle that the Haitian populace upholds. Whether one is a young businessperson who starts a business for the improvement of society through the creation of employment opportunities, a community leader getting people together to address a particular problem, or a school teacher who would like to see their students become successful in life, all the Haitian nationals have a common goal of wanting to make a positive change in society.

The Haitian people know that it is not about the fame and profitability of leaders, though the Haitians believe that everyone has talents and abilities from the Almighty God that should be used. Leaders are based on the Scripture of Matthew, which states that whosoever wants to become the greatest must become the servant of the others they want to lead, and their aim is to lead using their power and wealth to help those in society (King James Version,

2019). As was observed with the Haitian community adopting such a mentality of servant leadership, the community actively engaged in the change process as they motivated other people to support them as well (Johnson, 2021). These are the stories of men and women struggling to survive despite overwhelming odds; it is the story of success and selflessness as well as innovation amidst adversity. Their stories of success while facing adversity are indeed vivid proof that one has to focus on one's goal and calling rather than waste energy on those who do not believe. In the lively Haitian population, the individuals are cognizant of the fact that the road to change is not a smooth one, though they do not lose hope. Thus, one can admit that such people are motivated by deep-seated belief in themselves and the fact that they have something more significant to do than listen to "haters" and pessimists who do not see the hidden potential within their country (Beckett, 2020). Using their energy to do something productive that will help their community, they are causing a change that is making a difference in people's lives and encouraging others to step up.

Are you willing to Work Hard to Achieve the End Goal?

The Haitian community is not for the faint of heart when it comes to leadership and striving to be change agents in societies. The people of Haiti can grasp the inherent wisdom that for any lasting transformation, desire comes along with the source strength to match it. It is for this reason that this ethos is founded on the Haitian people's pragmatic perception of the tenets of hard work and productivity (Beckett, 2020). They understand that it is not about getting a break but the outcome of hard work, commitment, and even courage to push that bit extra. This mindset is not just a theory or a concept, which is, in other conditions, just a dream; it is a genuine model of living that is developed and included in society. The Haitian people draw positive motivation from such cases, which means that they can also get to powerful positions through their own efforts (Charles, 2020). It turned to the real-life narratives of people who managed to achieve so much against all the odds—an entrepreneur who started a business venture having practically nothing or social activity.

A clear idea that unites all these stories of success is that one can become a winner if he wants it in the most desirable way. The awareness that talent and outstanding skills are Halley important, but it is the readiness to work for hours, to take the challenge, and not to surrender that makes leaders and changemakers out of ordinary citizens of Haiti (Charles, 2020). The attitude toward work is not restricted to any occupation; it is ingrained in virtually every element of the lives of Haitian immigrants (Elusma et al., 2022). Whether it is a young man or a woman who opens a business venture, a teacher who aims at changing the lives of students, or a community activist who tries to steer the inhabitants of his community in a particular direction, the Haitian people are focused and extremely hard-working.

One vivid example of the hard-working spirit of the Haitian people can be traced back to their attitude toward education within the Haitian community. It is noteworthy to acknowledge the Haitian people's stance on the development of knowledge and skills as they strive for children and youth education. It takes the efforts of parents, teachers, and community members who engage in fundraising, lobbying, and coming up with programs to ensure that students are facilitated when in school (Guzmán et al., 2020). It is not the degree or the certificate that is sought, but it is the preparation of the next generation of leaders who will help bring change in Haiti (Johnson, 2021). Haitian people are fully aware that investing in the education and training of the young generation is investing in the future of the Haitian nation.

Irrespective of the nature of the business, Haitians never compromise on their hard work, especially in their education-based businesses. No matter if it is an art-based small business or a fast-moving start-up business, the Haitian people face the prospect of establishing and growing a successful business with tenacity. They do not blink at barriers that usually surround the start of new investments and enterprises: lack of capital, cumbersome regulations, or stiff competition (Johnson, 2021). While the situation makes it look like such people are challenged in their pursuit of success, they tap into their bucket of creativity, hard work, and endurance to defy such odds and make sound businesses that generate enough wealth. It is important to note that professionalism fused with a workaholic mentality is not the sole working lifestyle that influences the Haitian people; it defines how this nation functions on the civic and communal level (Guzmán et al., 2020). There is a strong culture of volunteering, activism, and good neighborliness amongst the Haitian people, especially those in the lower layers of the population pyramid, from citizens' groups to local authorities. From any campaign to clean the neighborhood, campaign for better infrastructure, or organizing resources to support families in need, Haitian people do this with the same passion as they do in their private and development endeavors. They know that leadership does not just mean getting to a position where one is better off but where one can be of value to society and help lift the standard of society. Undoubtedly, there is an element of dogmatic belief in the Haitian community's work ethic and the belief that the collective's endeavors can make a positive change. They also deduced that since they possess God-endowed talents and abilities, coupled with focus and hard work, any challenge can be conquered, and the future can be made prosperous, united, and impactful (Lowe, 2023). Indeed, this realistic, religious attitude to labor and success reflects many Haitian Americans who have gained the status of leaders in their spheres.

    A vivid example is Garcelle Beauvais, the talented actress and model who raises awareness about the situation in Haiti and encourages people to believe in themselves no matter what. Even when she has encountered many barriers and tensions in her work, Beauvais still has strong, unyielding beliefs about excellence and contributing to welfare. From her early days as a model and television personality to her recent roles in hit shows like "The Real Housewives of Beverly Hills" and "Spider-Man: Homecoming," Beauvais continues to work professionally, to be very persistent, and to work really hard; she enjoys the recognition of her peers and the fans (Lauren, 2021). Nevertheless, one cannot speak of Beauvais simply as an artist; she is also an active, loud voice for change for the Haitian people and the culture that promotes Haitian causes and gives her help to those who are trying to introduce real changes in the lives of Haitians both in Haiti and in immigrant communities (Lauren, 2021). With her charity and her passion, she remains a bright, shining example of the light Haitian Americans can be while being a living embodiment of the American dream of working hard with the overall aim of something more. Thus, as the Haitian community advances within the United States and other parts of the world, accepting this principle of work ethic and high achievements, they get a positive result from the impact of their work. People and societies previously struggling to find the strength to stand up to a horrible destiny that was put in front of them are now proudly walking together for a better future (Neufeldt & Janzen, 2020). The nation, in general, was subject to the hardships of poverty, inequality, and instability but now stands out as a shining example of what can be achieved when people are prepared to get down to business and work for the future (Naidu et al., 2021).

The Steps to Take to Rise and Shine in the Community

As the Haitian communities, full of life and energy, respond to the call and become leaders for change, they are aware that the path laid out shall not lack a solid plan and active steps to take in order to succeed. This is the most doable and sequential approach that stemmed from the people's consciousness of Haiti that change is not adopted through mere occurrence but through the consistent and persistent struggle for one's course (Naidu et al., 2021). The first significant stage is self-reflection and discernment. The Haitian people comprehend that in order for them to properly and meaningfully lead within their societies, they must first dedicate time to focus on one's self (Neufeldt & Janzen, 2020). This period of self-reflection is no longer a theoretical approach but a way of mapping one's ideals and goals against the realities on the ground within their neighborhoods.

Through this process of self-discovery, the people of Haiti can discover what they are gifted with, and then, after consulting with the leader and other important people in the society, they can figure out how to use these gifts to solve some of the problems. Thus, this enables an individual to get a vocation that fits them, and at the same time, it serves the purpose of society as well (Naidu et al., 2021). Another implication of Haitians accepting their destiny from God is that once the Haitian people understand their roles, which God intended them to fulfill, then there is a basis for the development of skills and the formation of expertise in the solution of problems affecting the communities (Miner & Bickerton, 2020). This can call for continuing with education to earn a higher degree or obtaining training forums that will enable them to acquire practical lessons that will enable them to effect the necessary change. An example of such a decision is a young Haitian-American who wants to become a community organizer and might decide to take a program that specializes in community organizing, administration of non-governmental organizations, and public policy (Trott et al., 2020). On the other hand, an ambitious individual may look for business incubation or any course that will assist in nurturing an idea, facilitate writing a business plan, and acquire the right mix of equipment required for translating a concept to reality (Salusky et al., 2020). As the people of Haiti go on with the socio-political rebuilding of their nation, they realize the need to forge alliances and partnerships. They also continuously look for opportunities to interact with other members of society and similar associations and authorities because people's power is known to work better than lone crusaders.

Haitian people work together through joint coordination and sourcing, which have been proven to unite and provide better results than if working in isolation. This sense of collectivism is perhaps most apparent in Haitians' handling of disasters and other forms of duress. Instead of facing these adversities individually, they exhibit solidarity and coordinate their efforts and assets for the purpose of helping one another, reconstructing their communities, and coming back even stronger (Miner & Bickerton, 2020). Additionally, faith is underlined as an important factor when Haitian community members talk about their leadership experience. Born and raised as people with faith in God, they truly understand that their source of strength and help is somewhere beyond this world, so they stay connected to it and ask for help, advice, and strength whenever they are faced with a problem (Lowe, 2023). This support is not only to help them endure the adversities that are inevitable in a leader's life, but it also gives their actions holy meaning and urges them to serve their callers with honor, mercy, and tenacity.

A shining example of such a Haitian-American positive image and integrated, faith-based approach to community leadership is Michaëlle Jean, who is the former Governor General of Canada and Secretary-General of the Organisation Internationale de la Francophonie (Fraser, 2023). Over the years, Jean has remained very passionate about advocating for the poor and vulnerable groups in and outside Canada (Fraser, 2023). After the destructive Haiti earthquake in January 2010, Jean has been actively involved in promoting assistance and the rebuilding process in her country, using her experience as an international publicist (Riverin-Coutlée & Harrington, 2022). She has also supported causes like women's and children's rights, young people, and sustainable development, and she has used her leadership to raise awareness about the struggles of the Haitian people and to mobilize people into action. It has been established that, at the center of Jean's leadership, there is a profound belief in the power of prayer and the almighty God, coupled with the understanding that change is possible only when people work hard, seek cooperation and partnerships, and care for the general good. For this reason, she has become the epitome of this sort of community development and motivation for other Haitian Americans who would also like to make a difference in improving the standards of their communities.

The Haitian people have come to realize that leadership is not all about fame or success. Instead, it is focused on leveraging earth-sourced capabilities and talents in order to improve the quality of people's lives (Fraser, 2023). The young talent that rises and evolves in their society takes time and effort to seek out and equip the upcoming talent with the knowledge and experiences they attain in their daily struggles. Thus, the Haitian community guarantees that the process of transformation is unending and passes from one generation to another, resulting in more improvements than deformities from the previous generation (Neufeldt & Janzen, 2020). Whether it is a long-time community activist working with a young mentee or an experienced businessperson donating to education to make the dreams of young business people turn into reality, the Haitian people are ready to continue leadership for generations to come.

SUMMARY OF THE BOOK

Introduction

The introduction looks at the issues affecting Haiti with an insight into the geographical location of the country, its historical background as the first independent black-controlled nation, and its present-day position as the poorest country in the Western Hemisphere. Haiti became an independent country in 1804 when slaves overthrew the French colonial masters, but reduced fortunes characterized the country for many decades up to this time due to various hardships like political instability, economic crises, and a regime of isolationism.

As a result of slavery in Haiti, formerly known as Saint-Domingue, Haiti experienced many of the issues that it has at the present time. War and slavery, economics in the form of the brutal plantation system, trade embargoes, and the money paid to France as indemnity for independence left behind long economic pains. Following this, Haiti has experienced a range of challenges, particularly the 2010 earthquake that was felt across the region. The text abounds with the necessity of raising future leaders' awareness of Haiti and its role in the context of globalization. It suggests that addressing Haiti's problems requires a multifaceted approach, including:

1. Passing information about Haiti and its problems as part of its past and present priorities
2. Trust-making between various groups in Haiti
3. Building from Haiti's cultural assets and post-quake gains
4. Delivering the Haitian brand and summing up the Haitian diaspora worldwide
5. Engaging the international community, NGOs, and the private sector
6. Creating awareness of diplomacy and negotiation as vital skills for solving conflicts.
7. Challenging conventional approaches to aid and targeting the approaches towards sustainable development

The introduction closes by insisting on the fact that a new generation of Haitian leaders is needed that is able to find and rally people on the basis of hope for a better change, participation in the world community, and other challenges that people face nowadays, and first of all, poverty and instability.

Glossary and Definitions:

1. Isolationism: The political policy where it is necessary to stay away from the affairs and interests of other groups, including the political affairs of other countries.

2. Indemnity: A definite amount of money that has been paid as remuneration or to cover losses.

3. Diaspora: Immigrants of different classes who, having migrated and settled in other regions of the world, have been dispersed from their place of original abode.

4. Non-governmental organizations (NGOs): organizations that are not owned by the government and that work for themselves.

5. Sustainable development: Development that aims at improving the quality of life now and into the future without overexploiting the resources of the planet.

6. Top-down aid paradigm: A paradigm of providing international assistance where most of the decisions and resources are provided by the donors and most of the choices to be met are provided by the recipient countries.

7. Sensitization: The act of creating a public opinion, making people recognize the existence of or react to specific ideas, incidents, or situations.

Chapter 1

Chapter 1 covers the topic of leadership, defining the meaning of leadership, the different classifications of leaders, the various leadership approaches, and the leadership controversy about nature versus nurture. Leadership is said to be the ability to influence people towards the accomplishment of a given purpose through the use of management direction, decision-making, and execution of decisions. Thus, the chapter insists on the fact that leadership goes beyond its classical organizational roles and is a process of change. It is a summary of the main elements relevant to leadership, such as visioning, communication, affective self-regulation, flexibility, and energization of others. When talking about leadership approaches in the text, one can mention autocratic, democratic, and laissez-faire, along with modern approaches such as transformational, transactional, and situational leadership. It emphasizes the fact that for leadership to be most effective in terms of people, it is vital that one is capable of transforming personalities for different settings and situations.

The chapter also describes the current controversy on the leadership trait, which is whether it is inborn or acquired. It gives the pros for each side, and in the end, it comes to the conclusion that leadership must be a blend of some people born with the traits and some acquired behavior. The text also underlines the fact that it is necessary to grow and change in leadership, no matter the genetic traits. In the chapter, ethical leadership, integrity, and actions that can create commitment and drive in others are highlighted repeatedly. It also has a connection with servant leadership, as described in the Bible, where Jesus Christ, being the example of a servant leader, succumbs to everything so as to lead others. The final section of the chapter stresses the importance of the study of leadership in educational institutions, organizations, and society in general. This way, it underlines the values of leadership training for any people and demands that leadership experiences should be provided to different individuals as leadership skills can be created and enhanced with time.

Glossary and Definitions

1. Leadership: The process of influencing people to fulfill common goals.
2. Vision: The ability to foresee and articulate future possibilities.
3. Emotional intelligence: The capacity to understand and manage one's own emotions and those of others.
4. Autocratic Leadership: A style where the leader makes decisions without consulting others.
5. Democratic Leadership: A style that encourages team participation in decision-making.
6. Transformational Leadership: A style focused on inspiring and motivating followers to exceed expectations.
7. Transactional Leadership: A style based on exchanges between leaders and followers, often involving rewards and punishments.
8. Situational Leadership: An approach that adapts leadership style based on the followers' development level and the situation.

9. Servant Leadership: A leadership philosophy focused on serving others and prioritizing their needs.//
10. Adaptive Leadership: The ability to lead and assist organizations in coping with complex challenges and change.

Chapter 2

The second chapter deals with "The Leader in Me" philosophy and Stephen Covey's "Seven Habits of Highly Effective People." The Leader in Me is a concept asserting leadership potential in every human being irrespective of age, culture, or social stratum. It seeks to empower persons to master their destiny, make proper choices, and change society for the better. This approach works on altering the locus of control from external to internal, and the major component is that of action-taking.

The chapter explores the seven habits outlined by Covey: being proactive, beginning with the end in mind, putting first things first, thinking win-win, seeking first to understand then to be understood, synergizing, and sharpening the saw. These habits are offered as a comprehensive way for individuals to improve who they are as people and as professionals, emphasizing understanding themselves, taking charge of their actions, thinking positively, and becoming better communicators.

The text explores how it is possible to apply such habits in community development and in building people. For example, being proactive in a complex setting means being assertive in a way that tries to solve problems that affect that given community. It assists in community visioning and goal setting, starting with the end in mind. Isolating the important items enables effective decision-making on which of the community projects need to be fulfilled first and priorities in resource allocation. The tactic makes everyone a winner has been used to encourage cooperation and facilitate positive interaction in the communities. The concept of seeking first to understand, then to be understood aims at underscoring the aspect of listening within the community discourse. Synergizing implies the notion of maximizing the community's effectiveness by employing different talents. In the context of focusing on the community, sharpening the saw' can be translated as investing in the enhancement of the community's assets. The chapter also exhibits scriptural support for each developed habit to show how they apply to different situations. It copes with difficulties in changing these habits and short-term thinking, which are the major obstacles to accomplishing this work, and underlines the positive outcomes of the long-term attitude.

Glossary and Definitions

1. Proactive: Taking initiative and responsibility for one's life and actions.
2. Synergy: The combined effect of collaboration that is greater than the sum of individual efforts.
3. Empathetic listening: Listening with the intent to understand, not just to reply.
4. Win-win: A mindset that seeks mutually beneficial solutions in all interactions.
5. Locus of control: The degree to which people believe they have control over their life outcomes.
6. Growth mindset: The belief that abilities and intelligence can be developed through effort and learning.
7. Self-leadership: The practice of intentionally influencing one's thinking, feelings, and behaviors to achieve one's objectives.

8. Community visioning: The process of creating a shared, long-term vision for a community's future.

Chapter 3

Chapter 3 focuses on the key characteristics and tasks of leadership within communities with a strong reference to scriptural provisions. It points out the fact that community leaders must act as servant leaders; hence, they must put the interests of the group before theirs. The most valued aspects are integrity, practical knowledge and decisions, fearlessness, empathy, and good management of communication. The chapter dealing with community challenges emphasizes the themes of teaching and learning throughout one's life, partnership, and teamwork. Thus, the text describes the options for participation in communities, including volunteering, voting, encouraging local businesses, being a positive role model for children, and initiating initiatives to arrange community events. They stress that it is in the interest of the people and advocate the Christian principles of love, service, and stewardship.

The chapter identifies the seven hats of a communal leader: a visionary, an administrator, a peacemaker, a lobbyist, a trainer, and a principal of resources. It emphasizes the need for harmony and cohesiveness by encouraging people and nations to identify with their communities, but also for readiness to fight calamities and hardships. The text offers principles on how people can effectively 'rise and shine,' that is, transform themselves in the context of their community and become responsible and productive members through personal development, learning, self-initiative, and networking. This encourages the readers to be role models always to help mold society, coach others, and employ special skills and knowledge in social transformation. The chapter also discusses the different opportunities for the improvement of communities, such as volunteering, starting up community projects, advocating, providing financial assistance, environmental conservation, as well as diversification. It is rich in such concepts as volunteer work, the main findings of attachment figure-youth mentoring, and the utilization of professional competencies to enhance the community. Finally, the text focuses on how to involve communities in projects, potential sources of vision, people suggested to participate, principles such as openness, and the importance of recognition. It also points out the implementation of technology and social media in enhancing the turnout while ensuring that the engagement is face-to-face.

Glossary and Definitions

1. Servant Leadership: A leadership approach that prioritizes serving others and the community over personal interests.

2. Stewardship: The responsible management and use of resources for the benefit of the community.

3. Civic Engagement: Active participation in the political and social processes of a community.

4. Social Capital: The networks of relationships and shared values that enable a community to function effectively.

5. Advocacy: Speaking or acting on behalf of a cause, policy, or group of people.

Chapter 4

In chapter four, ten biblical models of community development regarding Haitians are described with the purpose of covering many aspects of spiritual, economic, and social concern. Chapter four insists on evangelistic and spiritual awakening as basic methodologies due to the need to start with spiritual growth despite Vodou's impact on Haitian culture penetration. Education and literacy programs are identified as instruments of empowerment and include support to schools, adults, and those that aim at teaching separable languages in two languages. Presently, the learning material elaborates on healthcare and wellness programs as the components that meet critical medical concerns while offering care for people's souls. Considering the current chapter, client relations and economic empowerment, with an emphasis on job creation, microfinancing, vocational training, agriculture, and ethical trade, are also described in the text. Investment in societies' structures and infrastructures is underlined as a viable means of improving quality of life and growing economies. Writing and research propose social justice and advocacy as needed for the redressing of past injustices as well as for the solving of current issues affecting Haitian populations at home and in the diaspora. Preservation of the environment and conservation are introduced as crucial factors, relating biblical tenets on stewardship of God's creation to practical acts of environmentalism.

    Culture and arts are considered important assets in the retention of Haitian essence and strength, with special emphasis on communities that are scattered in different parts of the world. The concepts of youths and their mentors are presented as major topics that are essential for the formation of leaders and for the struggle against intergenerational issues. Last but not least, the concepts of reconciliation and transitional peacebuilding are also discussed as important procedures for rebuilding society with rifts. In all these paradigms presented in the chapter, references to the Bible are incorporated to support these community development approaches. As illustrated in the text, all of these strategies are integrated and may result in a comprehensive and long-lasting improvement of the Haitian communities.

Glossary and Definitions

1. Vodou: A syncretic religion practiced in Haiti, combining elements of West African Vodun, Roman Catholicism, and other spiritual traditions.
2. Diaspora: Populations of Haitians living outside of Haiti, often in countries such as the United States, Canada, and France.
3. Microfinance: Small-scale financial services, such as loans and savings accounts, are provided to individuals who lack access to traditional banking services.

4. WASH programs: Water, Sanitation, and Hygiene initiatives aimed at improving public health through better access to clean water and sanitation facilities.

5. Kompa: A popular music genre originating in Haiti, characterized by medium-to-fast tempo and mixed African and European influences.

6. Rara: A form of festival music that originated in Haiti, typically performed during Easter week celebrations.

7. Mizik Rasin: A musical movement in Haiti that combines elements of traditional Vodou ceremonial and folk music with modern instruments and styles.

8. Phronema ta eschatai: A Greek phrase meaning "peacemakers," referring to those who work towards reconciliation and peace.

Chapter 5

Chapter 5 focuses on the leadership culture that is present within Haitians from childhood to adulthood. It is important to note Haitians' belief that people are born as leaders, which is backed by the core belief of the people of Haiti that man is made in the image of God. Thus, this belief propels Haitians towards nurturing the talents they possess and giving back to society. The chapter underscores the ideas of risk management, passion for the chosen occupation even if people say that it is unprofitable, as well as determination and a hard-working attitude. It refers to them by such examples of prominent Haitian Americans like Wyclef Jean, Jean Michel Basquiat, and Edwidge Danticat, among others, with unique impacts that they portray to their communities. With regard to the Haitian perspective on leadership, it is important to point out that the role of a leader is presented in this text as a religious charge, one that the individuals must be endowed with courage, tenacity, and faith to undertake. It provides guidelines on who and how one has to become to fit into the leadership position; the steps involve self-auditing, acquiring certain skills and competence, strengthening partnerships, and spirituality. The chapter also presents information regarding the approach to Haiti to encompass community development that places emphasis on education, health, and economic uplift. As in any Haitian story, the focus placed upon servant leadership never wanes, in which the central value of success is not the upgrading of a person's status but the result of that elevation on the rest of society. The chapter closes with knowledge sharing and nurturing of the future leaders and transmitting of leadership values for the continual cycle of community change for the better.

Glossary and Definitions

1. Ethnoentrepreneurship: Business practices and attitudes specific to a particular ethnic group.
2. Diaspora: Relating to people who have moved away from their ancestral homeland.
3. Servant leadership: A leadership philosophy focused on serving others and prioritizing their needs.
4. Divine providence: The belief that God has a plan and intervenes in human affairs.
5. Community activism: Efforts to promote, direct, or intervene in social, political, economic, or environmental reform with the desire to make improvements in society.

References

Afrifa Jnr, S., &Dzogbewu, T. (2020). Goleman's intrapersonal dimension of emotional intelligence: Does it predict effective leadership? *Organizational Cultures: An International Journal*, *21*(2), 35–50. https://doi.org/10.18848/2327-8013/cgp/v21i02/35-50

Ahmad, J., Boon, Y., Noordin, M. K., Jambari, H., & Hamid, M. Z. A. (2022). Seven habits of highly effective people among school leaders in Riau islands, Indonesia. *International Journal of Health Sciences*, *1*(1), 8095–8100. https://doi.org/10.53730/ijhs.v6ns5.10808

Alexander, L. M. (2021). Black utopia: Haiti and black transnational consciousness in the early nineteenth century. *The William and Mary Quarterly*, *78*(2), 215. https://doi.org/10.5309/willmaryquar.78.2.0215

Andolina, M. W., & Conklin, H. G. (2021). Cultivating empathic listening in democratic education. *Theory & Research in Social Education*, *49*(3), 390–417.

https://doi.org/10.1080/00933104.2021.1893240

Anthony, B. (2023). The role of community engagement in urban innovation towards the co-creation of smart sustainable cities. *Journal of the Knowledge Economy, 1*(1), 1–33. https://doi.org/10.1007/s13132-023-01176-1

Banks, G. C., Dionne, S. D., Mast, M. S., & Sayama, H. (2022). Leadership in the digital era: A review of who, what, when, where, and why. *The Leadership Quarterly, 33*(5), 101634. https://doi.org/10.1016/j.leaqua.2022.101634

Barrow, M. (2022). Counter-Cultural-Memory: Performative strategies of arts management and cultural policy for the Caribbean. *Springer EBooks, 1*(1), 191–208. https://doi.org/10.1007/978-3-030-85810-0_12

Beckett, G. (2020). Unlivable life: Ordinary disaster and the atmosphere of crisis in Haiti. *Small Axe: A Caribbean Journal of Criticism, 24*(2), 78–95. https://doi.org/10.1215/07990537-8604502

Benmira, S., & Agboola, M. (2021). Evolution of leadership theory.

BMJ Leader, 5(1), 3–5. https://doi.org/10.1136/leader-2020-000296

Bhardwaj, A. (2022). Organizational culture and effective leadership in academic medical institutions. *Journal of Healthcare Leadership, 14*(1), 25–30. https://doi.org/10.2147/jhl.s358414

Boutros, A. (2020). "Sounds like Haiti": Haiti as muse in Canadian popular music. *Popular Music and Society, 44*(5), 1–19. https://doi.org/10.1080/03007766.2020.1732019

Bush, J. T. (2020). Win-win-lose? Sustainable HRM and the promotion of unsustainable employee outcomes. *Human Resource Management Review, 30*(3), 1–4. https://doi.org/10.1016/j.hrmr.2018.11.004

Charles, J. M. (2020). The slave revolt that changed the world and the conspiracy against it: The Haitian revolution and the birth of scientific racism. *Journal of Black Studies, 51*(4), 275–294. https://doi.org/10.1177/0021934720905128

Chen, J. K. C., &Sriphon, T. (2022). Authentic leadership, trust, and social exchange relationships under the influence of leader behavior. *Sustainability*, *14*(10), 1-32. https://doi.org/10.3390/su14105883

Ciorciari, J. D. (2022). Haiti and the pitfalls of sharing police powers. *International Peacekeeping*, *29*(3), 384–412. https://doi.org/10.1080/13533312.2022.2053286

Covey, S. R. (2004). *The 7 habits of highly effective people: Powerful lessons in personal change*. Free Press.

Deshommes, T., Nagel, C., Tucker, R., Dorcélus, L., Gautier, J., Koster, M. P., & Lechner, B. E. (2020). A quality improvement initiative to increase hand hygiene awareness and compliance in a neonatal intensive care unit in Haiti. *Journal of Tropical Pediatrics*, *67*(3), 1–4. https://doi.org/10.1093/tropej/fmaa029

Elusma, M., Tung, C., & Lee, C.-C. (2022). Agricultural drought risk assessment in the Caribbean region: The case of Haiti. *International Journal of Disaster Risk Reduction*, *83*(1), 1–4. https://doi.org/10.1016/j.ijdrr.2022.103414

Endrejat, P. C., & Burnes, B. (2022). Kurt lewin's ideas are alive! But why doesn't anybody recognize them? *Theory & Psychology, 32*(6), 931–952. https://doi.org/10.1177/09593543221118652

Fraser, G. (2023). Language, federalism and Canadian diplomacy. *Minorités Linguistiques et Société, 1*(20), 1–4. https://doi.org/10.7202/1094900ar

Fries, A., Kammerlander, N., &Leitterstorf, M. (2020). Leadership styles and leadership behaviors in family firms: A systematic literature review. *Journal of Family Business Strategy, 12*(1), 100374. https://doi.org/10.1016/j.jfbs.2020.100374

Garay, U., Pérez, E., Casanova, J., &Kratohvil, M. (2022). Color intensity, luminosity, contrast and art prices: The case of jean-michelbasquiat. *Academia RevistaLatinoamericana de Administración, 35*(3), 303–328. https://doi.org/10.1108/arla-05-2021-0110

Gardner, W. L., Lowe, K. B., Meuser, J. D., Noghani, F., Gullifor, D. P., &Cogliser, C. C. (2020). The leadership trilogy: A review of the third decade of the leadership quarterly. *The*

Leadership Quarterly, 31(1), 101379.

https://doi.org/10.1016/j.leaqua.2019.101379

Gonçalves, S. P., Vieira dos Santos, J., Figueiredo-Ferraz, H., Gil-Monte, P. R., & Carlotto, M. S. (2022). Editorial: Occupational health psychology: From burnout to well-being at work. *Frontiers in Psychology, 13*(1), 1–5. https://doi.org/10.3389/fpsyg.2022.1069318

Guzmán, J. C., Schuenke-Lucien, K., D'Agostino, A. J., Berends, M., & Elliot, A. J. (2020). Improving reading instruction and students' reading skills in the early grades: Evidence from a randomized evaluation in Haiti. *Reading Research Quarterly, 56*(1), 173–193. https://doi.org/10.1002/rrq.297

Huang, Z., Sindakis, S., Aggarwal, S., & Thomas, L. (2022). The role of leadership in collective creativity and innovation: Examining academic research and development environments. *Frontiers in Psychology, 13*(13), 1–18. https://doi.org/10.3389%2Ffpsyg.2022.1060412

Jarad, N. A., Ahmad, J., Tahir, L. M., &Jambari, H. (2020). A study of the seven habits among teachers of highly educated and motivated people in government schools in Palestine. *Edukasi*, *14*(2), 100–108.

https://doi.org/10.15294/edukasi.v14i2.27181

Johnson, R. A. (2021). Haiti and the United States: In black print. *Atlantic Studies*, *1*(1), 1–18.

https://doi.org/10.1080/14788810.2020.1798207

Jones, K. (2022). Leading professional learning: How can a journal take a leadership role? *Professional Development in Education*, *48*(2), 181–184.

https://doi.org/10.1080/19415257.2022.2042654

Kanat-Maymon, Y., Elimelech, M., & Roth, G. (2020). Work motivations as antecedents and outcomes of leadership: Integrating self-determination theory and the full range leadership theory. *European Management Journal*, *38*(4), 555–564. https://doi.org/10.1016/j.emj.2020.01.003

Karim, A., Bakhtiar, A., Sahrodi, J., & Chang, P. H. (2022). Spiritual leadership behaviors in religious workplace: The case of *pesantren*. *International Journal of Leadership in Education*, *1*(1), 1–29. https://doi.org/10.1080/13603124.2022.2076285

King James Version. (2019). *The holy bible*. BookRix.

Klarman, M., Schon, J., Cajusma, Y., Maples, S., Beau de Rochars, V. E. M., Baril, C., & Nelson, E. J. (2021). Opportunities to catalyse improved healthcare access in pluralistic systems: A cross-sectional study in Haiti. *BMJ Open*, *11*(11), 1–4. https://doi.org/10.1136/bmjopen-2020-047367

Kowalski, M. J., Elliot, A. J., Guzman, J. C., & Schuenke-Lucien, K. (2022). Early literacy skill development and motivation in the low-income context of Haiti. *International Journal of Educational Research*, *113*(1), 101972. https://doi.org/10.1016/j.ijer.2022.101972

Kump, B. (2023). Lewin's field theory as a lens for understanding incumbent actors' agency in sustainability transitions. *Environmental Innovation and Societal Transitions*, *46*(1), 100683. https://doi.org/10.1016/j.eist.2022.11.008

Lansing, A. E., Romero, N. J., Siantz, E., Silva, V., Center, K., Casteel, D., & Gilmer, T. (2023). Building trust: Leadership reflections on community empowerment and engagement in a large urban initiative. *BMC Public Health*, *23*(1), 1–25.

https://doi.org/10.1186/s12889-023-15860-z

Lantagne, D., Lehmann, L., Yates, T., Gallandat, K., Sikder, M., Domini, M., & String, G. (2021). Lessons learned from conducting six multi-country mixed-methods effectiveness research studies on water, sanitation, and hygiene (WASH) interventions in humanitarian response. *BMC Public Health*, *21*(1), 3–5. https://doi.org/10.1186/s12889-021-10597-z

Lauren, A. (2021, April 27). *Real Housewives of Beverly Hills star Garcelle Beauvais talk about life at home and the new season of the show*. Forbes. https://www.forbes.com/sites/amandalauren/2021/04/27/real-housewives-of-beverly-hills-star-garcelle-beauvais-talks-life-at-home-and-the-new-season-of-the-show/

Lowe, L. J. (2023). Where have all the oungangone?: Charismatic christianity and moral representations of vodou in Haiti. *Nova Religio the Journal of Alternative and Emergent Religions*, *26*(4), 8–32. https://doi.org/10.1525/nr.2023.26.4.8

Miner, M., & Bickerton, G. (2020). A new model of christian

leadership: Insights from the job demands–resources model and trinitarian theology. *Journal of Psychology and Theology, 48*(4), 2–5.

https://doi.org/10.1177/0091647120908010

Minn, P. (2020). Capturing kontredans: The transnational exposure of a haitian dance form. *Latin American and Caribbean Ethnic Studies, 15*(4), 1–21.

https://doi.org/10.1080/17442222.2020.1831155

Mombeuil, C. (2020). Institutional conditions, sustainable energy, and the UN sustainable development discourse: A focus on Haiti. *Journal of Cleaner Production, 254*(1), 1–4.

https://doi.org/10.1016/j.jclepro.2020.120153

Naidu, S., Robinson, J. A., & Young, L. E. (2021). Social origins of dictatorships: Elite networks and political transitions in Haiti. *American Political Science Review, 115*(3), 1–17.

https://doi.org/10.1017/s0003055421000289

Neufeldt, R. C., & Janzen, R. (2020). Learning from and with community-based and participatory action research: Constraints and adaptations in a youth-peacebuilding initiative in Haiti. *Action Research*, *19*(1), 1–4. https://doi.org/10.1177/1476750320916226

Ospina, S. M., Foldy, E. G., Fairhurst, G. T., & Jackson, B. (2020). Collective dimensions of leadership: Connecting theory and method. *Human Relations*, *73*(4), 441–463. https://doi.org/10.1177/0018726719899714

Pawar, A., Sudan, K., Satini, S., &Sunarsi, D. (2020). Organizational servant leadership. *International Journal of Educational Administration, Management, and Leadership*, *1*(2), 63–76. https://doi.org/10.51629/ijeamal.v1i2.8

Pellegrini, M. M., Ciampi, F., Marzi, G., & Orlando, B. (2020). The relationship between knowledge management and leadership: Mapping the field and providing future research avenues. *Journal of Knowledge Management*, *24*(6), 1445–1492. https://doi.org/10.1108/JKM-01-2020-0034

Porfírio, J. A., Carrilho, T., Felício, J. A., & Jardim, J. (2020). Leadership characteristics and digital transformation. *Journal of Business Research*, *124*(1), 610–619. https://www.sciencedirect.com/science/article/pii/S01482963

Riverin-Coutlée, J., & Harrington, J. (2022). Phonetic change over the career: A case study. *Linguistics Vanguard, 8*(1), 2–4. https://doi.org/10.1515/lingvan-2021-0122

Salam, M. A., & Khan, S. A. (2020). Lessons from the humanitarian disaster logistics management. *Benchmarking: An International Journal, 27*(4), 1455–1473. https://doi.org/10.1108/bij-04-2019-0165

Salusky, I., Tull, M., Case, A. D., & Soto-Nevarez, A. (2020). Fostering well-being through social support: The role of evangelical communities in the lives of dominican women of Haitian descent. *American Journal of Community Psychology, 67*(1-2), 205–219. https://doi.org/10.1002/ajcp.12467

Siangchokyoo, N., Klinger, R. L., & Campion, E. D. (2020). Follower transformation as the linchpin of transformational leadership theory: A systematic review and future research agenda. *The Leadership Quarterly, 31*(1), 101341.

Song, Z., Li, W.-D., Jin, X., Ying, J., Zhang, X., Song, Y., Li, H., & Fan, Q. (2022). Genetics, leadership position, and well-being: An investigation with a large-scale GWAS. *Proceedings of the National Academy of Sciences*, *119*(12), 1–4. https://doi.org/10.1073/pnas.2114271119

Tayfur Ekmekci, O., Metin Camgoz, S., Guney, S., & Kemal Oktem, M. (2021). The mediating effect of perceived stress on transformational and passive-avoidant, leadership-commitment linkages. *International Journal of Organizational Leadership*, *10*(4), 348–366. https://doi.org/10.33844/ijol.2021.60595

Tench, P. J., Green, R., Tsemunhu, R., Nobles, K., Truby, W., & Brockmeier, L. (2021). FranklinCovey leader in me program: The impact on quality of work life and perceived relationship changes between administrators and teachers. *National Youth Advocacy and Resilience Journal*, *5*(1), 28–49. https://doi.org/10.20429/nyarj.2021.050103

Todnem, R. (2021). Leadership: In pursuit of purpose. *Journal of Change Management*, *21*(1), 1–15. tandfonline.

https://doi.org/10.1080/14697017.2021.1861698

Trott, C. D., Rockett, M. L., Gray, E.-S., Lam, S., Even, T. L., & Frame, S. M. (2020). "Another Haiti starting from the youth": Integrating the arts and sciences for empowering youth climate justice action in Jacmel, Haiti. *Community Psychology in Global Perspective, 6*(2/2), 48–70. https://doi.org/10.1285/i24212113v6i2-2p48

Viana Feranita, N., Nugraha, A., & Andrean Sukoco, S. (2020). Effect of transformational and transactional leadership on smes in indonesia. *Problems and Perspectives in Management, 18*(3), 415–425. https://doi.org/10.21511/ppm.18(3).2020.34

Villares, E., Miller, A. E., & Chevalier, J. (2023). The impact of leader in me on the school climate and student behaviors: A meta-analysis. *International Journal of Education Policy and Leadership, 19*(2), 1–16. https://doi.org/10.22230/ijepl.2023v19n2a1339

Wallerstein, N., Oetzel, J. G., Sanchez-Youngman, S., Boursaw, B., Dickson, E., Kastelic, S., Koegel, P., Lucero, J. E., Magarati,

M., Ortiz, K., Parker, M., Peña, J., Richmond, A., & Duran, B. (2020). Engage for equity: A long-term study of community-based participatory research and community-engaged research practices and outcomes. *Health Education & Behavior, 47*(3), 380–390. https://doi.org/10.1177/1090198119897075

Williamson, O., Swann, C., Bennett, K. J. M., Bird, M. D., Goddard, S. G., Schweickle, M. J., & Jackman, P. C. (2022). The performance and psychological effects of goal setting in sport: A systematic review and meta-analysis. *International Review of Sport and Exercise Psychology, 1*(1), 1–29. https://doi.org/10.1080/1750984x.2022.2116723

Wilson. (2020). Fear, love, and leadership: Posing a machiavellian question to the hebrew bible. *Journal of Biblical Literature, 139*(2), 233-253. https://doi.org/10.15699/jbl.1392.2020.1

Wilson, R., Joiner, K., & Abbasi, A. (2021). Improving students' performance with time management skills. *Journal of University Teaching and Learning Practice, 18*(4), 230–250. https://doi.org/10.53761/1.18.4.16

Wuryani, E., Rodli, A. F., Sutarsi, S., Dewi, N. N., & Arif, D. (2021). Analysis of decision support system on situational leadership styles on work motivation and employee performance. *Management Science Letters, 11*(2), 365–372. http://dx.doi.org/10.5267/j.msl.2020.9.033

Yi, C. (2021). The bloomsbury handbook to edwidgedanticat. *Contemporary Women's Writing, 15*(3), 423–424. https://doi.org/10.1093/cww/vpab015

Yuriev, A., Dahmen, M., Paillé, P., Boiral, O., &Guillaumie, L. (2020). Pro-environmental behaviors through the lens of the theory of planned behavior: A scoping review. *Resources, Conservation and Recycling, 155*(1), 1–4. https://doi.org/10.1016/j.resconrec.2019.104660

OTHER BOOKS

Gedeon, Wadner, Hope for the new generation, Langhorne, PA. H.G. Publishing, 2009

Gedeon, Wadner, Espoir pour la nouvelle génération, Philadelphia, PA, Createspace Publishing, 2017

Gedeon, Wadner, Prayer is the solution, Philadelphia, PA. Createspace Publishing, 2019

Gedeon, Wadner, La prière est la solution, Philadelphia, PA. Createspace Publishing, 2019

Gedeon, Wadner, Walking into God's purpose for your life, Philadelphia, PA. Sentinel Publishing, 2024

Gedeon, Wadner, Comment réaliser le plan de Dieu pour votre vie, Sentinel Publishing, 2024

Contact :

Pour vos séminaires, ateliers et invitations, veuillez contacter l'auteur par l'un des courriels suivants :

Adresse électronique :
Wadnergedeon@gmail.com
Pastorwadner@gmail.com
Site web : www.WadnerGedeon.com

Healing a nation: Leadership, Faith and Community in Haiti's Journey Forward

Healing a nation: Leadership, Faith and Community in Haiti's Journey Forward

Healing a nation: Leadership, Faith and Community in Haiti's Journey Forward

Healing a nation: Leadership, Faith and Community in Haiti's Journey Forward

Made in the USA
Columbia, SC
09 November 2024

0f347543-823d-4b9e-a5d3-2662c915d8bcR01